Essential
Berlin

by

GABRIELLE MACPHEDRAN
and
ADAM HOPKINS

Gabrielle MacPhedran, a journalist and broadcaster,
has written several *Essential* guides
together with Adam Hopkins,
a travel writer and regular contributor
to the London *Daily Telegraph*.

Little, Brown and Company
Boston   Toronto   London

FIRST U.S. EDITION

The contents of this publication are believed correct at the time of printing.
Nevertheless, the publishers cannot accept responsibility for errors or
omissions, nor for changes in details given. We are always grateful to readers
who let us know of any errors or omissions they come across, and future
printings will be updated accordingly.

Produced by the Publishing Division of The Automobile Association of Great
Britain.

Written by Gabrielle MacPhedran and Adam Hopkins
"Peace and Quiet" section by Paul Sterry
Series Adviser: Ingrid Morgan
Series Controller: Nia Williams

ISBN 0-316-25038-4

10 9 8 7 6 5 4 3 2 1

PRINTED IN TRENTO, ITALY

This book employs a
simple rating system to
help choose which
places to visit:

◆◆◆   do not miss

◆◆   see if you can

◆   worth seeing if
       you have time

INTRODUCTION

Berlin – one of the world's great cities. Berlin – where disaster and division, symbolised by the Wall that split the city, have recently yielded to some kind of reconciliation. Berlin – once more itself, whole and entire since German reunification in 1990, yet physically and mentally marked, first by the destruction of World War II and now by more than 40 years in which two different systems of politics, two different economies, two different ideologies, two different nations, existed side by side in the same city. Once it seemed that this rivalry of systems might lead to a new World War, with Berlin as the flashpoint. Now the consequences may still be seen during a walk through the city, with brash capitalism on one side and on the other the drab and dusty remnants of a socialism that has been an admitted failure.

That is one reason for visiting Berlin. Those who take the historical approach will go further, for this was the city of Hitler's Third

An enduring symbol: Brandenburger Tor expressed Prussian Imperialism, Cold War conflict, and finally freedom

Reich, military aggressor turned victim of a war it had itself provoked. Before that it was the focus of the Weimar Republic, scene of frenzied inflation, intellectual ferment, worker politics and naughty nightclubs. Before that again, it was the capital of an empire with military parades and brisk efficiency on one hand, and a chaotic, teeming, discontented industrial metropolis on the other. Through all this Berlin emerged not just as one of the great capitals of Europe but also one of the cultural capitals of the world. It has world-class museums and living culture, too – theatre, opera, satire, writing, painting, an annual Film Festival of considerable prestige and magnificent classical music-making. Add to this again great energy in jazz and rock music and a tradition by which live music may be heard at hundreds of Berlin pubs, any night of the week, right through the night.

The other main reason for visiting Berlin is the unique atmosphere in the former West. Because of its isolation and the strangeness of its situation, West Berlin developed an informality quite different from that of other German cities. Citizens of the old West were free from the draft, a fact which combined with the general tolerance as an attraction for young people. West Berlin was an 'alternative' city. Mostly, this created a sense of comfort, but there were also pockets of extreme radicalism. Their existence led at times to undoubted excesses, with disputes over squatting, for example, turning into pitched battles. At the same time, however, it was the prevalence of squatting which helped to preserve many pre-war buildings, calamitously run down during the 1960s and 1970s and in real danger of demolition. These are now being done up, often by former squatters still living in them, and are seen as a unique part of the city's heritage. Another distinctive element of West Berlin has been the presence of 'guest workers', the vast majority of them Turkish, who came during the 1950s and 1960s. Never well assimilated, and still conspicuously poorer than the rest of the population, they lead a separate semi-submerged life, entering the mainstream

East still meets West in Berlin at Maybachufer's Turkish Market

mainly in the provision of instant food stalls. Problems exist, undoubtedly, and several questions arise for the 1990s. First, will the East itself become an alternative city? Or will it on the contrary be undermined by a new briskness, even perhaps aggression? It is precisely questions of this kind, allied to Berlin's history and culture, which make a trip so fascinating at present.

Berlin Today

Berlin, with just four million people, is an enormous city, covering huge tracts of land. Within its boundaries, both to east and west, lie large lakes and considerable forests. Even in the centre there are large open areas such as the Tiergarten, one-time hunting ground of princes, and the city is pierced by rivers and laced with canals. Great chunks of it, however, are extremely urban; and almost everything is new, due to the shocking extent of its ruination during and after World War II. Amid the newness and rawness, there are some formidable survivals. Two whole residential districts – Kreuzberg in the West and Prenzlauer Berg in the East – retain the shape if not the feel of 19th-century Berlin. Even more important in the look of the city has been the fragmentary survival followed

*Bebelplatz, off
Unter den Linden,
is a surviving
enclave of the
Hohenzollern city*

by total reconstruction, of a large sequence of
the principal buildings of Prussian and
Imperial Berlin, running up the great city
centre thoroughfare of Unter den Linden, a
name whose literal meaning is Under the
Linden Trees. It is here that you really feel at
the heart of Berlin. The other place where
that used to be true was at the Berlin Wall,
which, mostly vanished now, wriggled its way
until 1989–90 across the centre. The Wall, in
German Die Mauer, was built in 1961 to
prevent East Germans moving to the West, as
many thousands were doing annually. Its
disappearance has left a swathe of dead
ground right across the middle of the city.
The line taken by the Wall followed the line of
division at the end of the war in 1945. The
historic centre of Berlin was the borough
called Mitte ('Middle'), and that fell entirely
on the eastern side. It includes the grand
processional way of Unter den Linden;
Museumsinsel (Museum Island), with its
cathedral and extraordinary museums; and
Alexanderplatz, one-time meeting point for all
Berlin.

West Berlin developed a new focus around the Kaiser-Wilhelm-Gedächtniskirche. This imposing neo-Gothic building was ruined in World War II and left in its ruined state as a perpetual reminder. The open space beside the church is called the Breitscheidplatz, and has become a haven for hippies, tourists, ice-cream eaters and people taking photographs or staging protests. On the far side of the church, the Kurfürstendamm, or Ku'damm, runs away in a westerly direction, with cinemas, brightly lit shops and endlessly flowing crowds.

Most people stay in this area, even today, and use it as a launching pad in their exploration of Berlin. Nearby Zoo Station is still probably the city's best focus of communication, with large numbers of buses converging here, as well as the S-Bahn and the U-Bahn, Berlin's underground railway system. These easy transportation connections will also take the visitor out of the city centre into the surrounding area of lakes and woods, and southwest to Potsdam, palace-city of Brandenburg and the Prussian monarch.

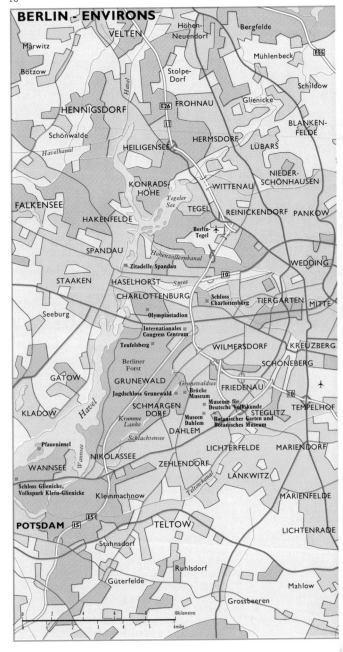

BERLIN - ENVIRONS

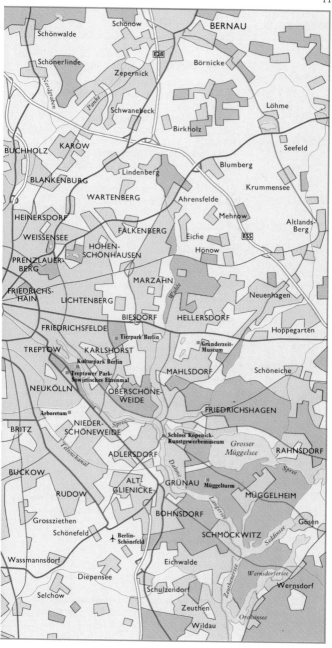

Schönow

BERNAU

Schönwalde

Schönerlinde

Börnicke

E28

Zepernick

Löhme

Schwanebeck

Birkholz

BUCHHOLZ

KAROW

Seefeld

Lindenberg

Blumberg

BLANKENBURG

Krummensee

WARTENBERG

Ahrensfelde

HEINERSDORF

Mehrow

Altlands-
Berg

WEISSENSEE

FALKENBERG

Eiche

E55

HÖHEN-
SCHÖNHAUSEN

Hönow

PRENZLAUER-
BERG

MARZAHN

Wuhle

FRIEDRICHS-
HAIN

Neuenhagen

LICHTENBERG

BIESDORF

HELLERSDORF

Hoppegarten

FRIEDRICHSFELDE

Tierpark Berlin

Gründerzeit-
Museum

TREPTOW

KARLSHORST

Kulturpark Berlin

MAHLSDORF

Schöneiche

Treptower Park-
Sowjetisches Ehrenmal

NEUKÖLLN

OBERSCHÖNE-
WEIDE

FRIEDRICHSHAGEN

Arboretum

Spree

BRITZ

NIEDER-
SCHÖNEWEIDE

Schloss Köpenick-
Kunstgewerbemuseum

Grosser
Müggelsee

RAHNSDORF

ADLERSDORF

Dahme

Spree

BUCKOW

Teltowkanal

ALT-
GLIENICKE

GRÜNAU

Müggelturm

MÜGGELHEIM

RUDOW

BOHNSDORF

Langersee

Grossziethen

Berlin-
Schönefeld

Gösen

Schönefeld

SCHMÖCKWITZ

Seddinsee

Wassmannsdorf

Eichwalde

Wernsdorferfsee

Diepensee

Zeuthenersee

Wernsdorf

Selchow

Schulzendorf

Zeuthen

Oder-Spree

Wildau

BACKGROUND

Berlin is young in European terms. Little
development took place here till the early
Middle Ages.

Hunter-gatherers passed through in dim
antiquity, leaving little mark among the
forests, lakes and sandy wastes of the country
that later acquired the name of Brandenburg.
Scattered farmers settled in the Stone Age.
The Romans were delighted to pass it up,
penetrating only into the south and west of
what later became Germany.

Amidst the wild scenery of Brandenburg –
which today is deeply loved and prized –
settlements slowly developed. Two of these
were on either side of the River Spree,
covering in due course a long, low island in
the middle. The settlements were named
Berlin and Cölln, and the island is the very
one where a royal palace and museums were
later to grow up.

Berlin and Cölln were eastward-looking,
river-trading towns and grew important
enough by the 13th century to receive their
own charters. In 1307, they combined to build
a joint town hall. There were already two
churches, and one, the Marienkirche, hardly
damaged in the war, still stands. Castles were
erected, to northwest and southeast, on key
sites on the waterways, and later came to act
almost as gateways to the city. Their names
were Spandau and Köpenick, both since
replaced by later buildings – in Spandau a
fortress-citadel, in Köpenick a modest palace.
Otherwise, little survives of the older period,
except for small collections here and there in
museums, of the craft artefacts that were such
a brilliant feature of medieval German towns
and cities.

Beginnings of Greatness

The Germans were a community of the
loosest kind, defined by a language and in
due course the Christian religion (in which a
good deal of forest magic still remained). As
the Roman Empire faded, the Frankish
empire of Charlemagne and his descendants
rose to take its place. Little by little, this
transmuted itself into a German Empire

Marienkirche is a monument to the faith and wealth of the medieval city

stretching right across central Europe. It was elective, not hereditary and went by the name of the Holy Roman Empire of the German Nation. Brandenburg was part of it, a 'Mark' or border territory. In 1356 it was decided that seven German rulers should act as the chief electors of the German emperor. One of these was to be the ruler of the Mark of Brandenburg, known henceforward as the Elector of Brandenburg.

Berlin and Cölln, meanwhile, had joined the Hanseatic League of trading cities and showed a remarkable sense of independence. It took many a contest between the Hohenzollern family – from whom the Electors of Brandenburg were drawn – before the towns' independence was finally suppressed.

BACKGROUND

It was not until the 17th century, during the long reign of the Great Elector, Friedrich Wilhelm I (1620–88), that Brandenburg began to surface as a real power. Growing, industrious Berlin and a princely Potsdam a short way southwest became a kind of dual focus. Under Friedrich Wilhelm and particularly his son Friedrich III, stately baroque buildings were erected. In Potsdam, from 1660, a great Stadtschloss or Town Palace began to go up. In Berlin, as well as a palace on the island, a magnificent Arsenal was constructed on Unter den Linden, with contributions from Andreas Schlüter, first of a chain of outstanding Berlin architects and sculptors. A little way out of the city, though now in the city centre, the pretty palace of Charlottenburg went up for Sophie Charlotte, wife of Friedrich III.

Another big change in the period was the arrival of thousands of Huguenot craftsmen, persecuted in France but welcomed by Friedrich Wilhelm. Fragments of French still survive in Berlin dialect, and the Huguenots' cemetery (the Alte Französiche Friedhof) is an interesting place to visit. It lies along an improbable-looking lane through a housing development, by the tram terminal on the corner of Pflugstrasse and Wöhlerstrasse.

To Prussia with luggage: many French emigrées found work in the city

Prussian Berlin

Friedrich III crowned himself King of Prussia in 1701, and became Friedrich I of the new state. This was a critical moment, making Prussia the power base of the German-speaking peoples, with Berlin as their focus, rather than Vienna (main city of the old Holy Roman Empire).

Friedrich I's son, Wilhelm Friedrich I of Prussia, the so-called Soldier-King (1688–1740), carried the process further, organising a bureaucracy – one of the chief features of Prussia's later dominance – and building up an army. This was somewhat weakened by his predilection for giants, sought out all over Europe as his guardsmen and sometimes sent to him as human gifts by other rulers. The Soldier-King was odd in other ways as well. He had a savage temper, not far short of madness, and carried a swagger stick with which he would attack those who irritated him, cracking teeth and breaking noses. He made ferocious efforts to repress his son, later Friedrich II (1712–1786, king from 1740), known as Frederick the Great.

Young Friedrich, as crown prince, tried to escape from his father and was imprisoned for military desertion. His closest friend, most

probably his lover, was executed before his eyes. Succeeding to the throne, however, Friedrich carried on his father's tradition of efficiency and militarism, using Unter den Linden, and much of the remainder of the city centre, as a kind of glorified parade ground. Simultaneously, he plunged Prussia into the vortex of the European power struggle, and provoked the rest of Europe into challenging him in the bitter Seven Years War (1756–63). During this, Berlin was briefly occupied.

By the time he died Friedrich had made Prussia the leading state of continental Europe. On Unter den Linden, he built the Berlin Opera House (all attendance was by royal invitation). In Potsdam, he created the brilliant small-scale palace of Sanssouci and lived there, in all-male company, speaking in French and passing his time with luminaries such as Voltaire.

After his death, the declining strength of Prussia was no match for the might of Napoleon. Following a humiliating defeat at Jena, Berliners had to watch Napoleon come riding in triumph into the Prussian capital, under the Brandenburg Gate.

The French era was brief and made little impression. But after the Prussian restoration in 1815 it was clear that reform was now in order in Berlin. Army and bureaucracy were tightened up and strengthened. The two Humboldt brothers, both trained in the Prussian civil service, emerged to become symbolic founding fathers of a great Berlin academic tradition. Alexander (1769–1859) was the greatest naturalist and explorer of his day; Wilhelm (1767–1835) created the Humboldt University, which shone like a beacon in Berlin until the time of Hitler. The philosopher Hegel taught there; so did Albert Einstein.

It is no accident at all that Berlin has continuously produced a stunning range of intellectual achievement, right across the sciences and the arts, including architecture. The neo-classical buildings of Karl Friedrich Schinkel (1781–1819), also a romantic painter, contribute especially to the city's special character today. There is a Schinkel Museum

Humboldt University, where students have studied Hegel's dialectics and Einstein's theory of relativity

just off Unter den Linden at the Museumsinsel end. Berlin has also been a great generator of style, starting in the 1830s with the evolution of that comfortable type of furniture and décor known as Biedermeier.

The dominant figure of late 19th-century Prussia was Count Otto von Bismarck, a member of Prussia's Junker aristocracy who became a civil servant and eventually Prime Minister in Berlin. Under his guidance, Prussia smashed the armies of Austria in 1866, and was thus able to unite the northern German people into a nation-state for the first time, in 1871.

Heavy industries began making their mark on

Berlin from the middle of the 19th century.
The great Borsig plant, which made rails and
locomotives, features in many contemporary
paintings and is now a national monument.
By the end of the century, electricity had
arrived, and it was above all the demand for
electrical goods which fuelled the industries
of Berlin. Siemens, for example, had its
origins at about this time.

Hundreds of thousands of the rural poor
flocked in from Brandenburg and further east
to work in the new industries. The newcomers
were housed in huge tenements, consisting of
courtyard behind courtyard, often grand on
the exterior but progressively dreary in their
deeper recesses and sometimes with the
factory in the same complex. An intensely
lived slum life grew up in the Berlin
tenements and alleys, with its own distinctive
dialect.

Workers, increasingly unionised, called for
greater political and economic freedom, but
met nothing but repression. Here were to be
found the roots of German socialism and it

*The iron fist
emerged from the
velvet glove when
cavalry attacked
rioters in 1892*

was here, among the labouring masses of
Berlin and the German cities, that Karl Marx
believed the Revolution would begin. Berlin
boroughs such as Wedding and Moabit were

the centre for this vigorous, dissident,
proletarian life.
This was also the time of Jugendstil – the
German version of Art Nouveau – and the
best city blocks mix solid grandeur with its
decorative playfulness. Meanwhile, the
intellectual life of the city carried on
unabated.

The Weimar Years
World War I came as a catastrophe for
Germany. Berlin itself was never enthusiastic,
except in the first heady days of hostilities.
Popular demands for peace were matched by
demands for social justice, for a new
constitution, freedom, equality and socialism.
Kaiser Wilhelm II delayed, then abdicated in
1918. A new Republic was proclaimed from
the balcony of the Reichstag and a
government of the Social Democratic Party
was formed. At the same time, the
revolutionary leader, Karl Liebknecht,
proclaimed a rival, revolutionary Republic
from the balcony of the royal palace. The
official government brought in elite bands of
the army and specially formed, right-wing
units called the Freikorps, funded by
industrialists. Whole areas of Berlin were in
the grip of revolution, demanding a
Communist system of organisation. Karl
Liebknecht and his fellow-leader Rosa
Luxemburg were captured by the Freikorps
and shot. Rosa Luxemburg's body was
dumped in the Landwehr Canal. A plaque
now marks the spot. In the end, the revolution
failed. Berlin nevertheless remained a hotbed
of radical sentiment.
The new system of government, under
constant attack from both the left and right,
acquired the name of the Weimar Republic.
In Berlin, an attempted right-wing coup – the
Kapp putsch – was defeated by a left-wing
general strike. In 1923 a right-wing politician
named Adolph Hitler also failed in an
attempted coup – in Munich – and was briefly
imprisoned. Worker restlessness meanwhile
terrified the ruling classes.
Throughout these years, Germany staggered
under the humiliation both of a crushing

defeat and an impossible burden of war reparations. Soon the country experienced the world's first episode of hyperinflation, with cartloads of money required to buy a cabbage. Some relief, though, was on the way. Fearful of Communist revolution, the Americans now made an effort to aid economic recovery through the so-called Dawes Plan. Even so, the situation was dire, with millions out of work and no such thing as unemployment benefit. Many of the people, in Berlin as elsewhere, were close to starving.

Paradoxically, 1920s Berlin was also a time and a place unrivalled for freedom and creativity. What came to be known as the 'Weimar Culture' was marked by a level of high achievement in virtually every field, whether scientific or artistic. A tiny sample of Berlin's high achievers would produce names like Thomas and Heinrich Mann, Rainer Maria Rilke and Erich Kästner in literature; Bertolt Brecht and Erwin Piscator, Kurt Weill and Max Rheinhardt in theatre; George Grosz, John Heartfield and Käthe Kollwitz as artists committed to political comment and satire; Arnold Schönberg, Otto Klemperer and Wilhelm Furtwängler in music; Fritz Lang, Joseph von Sternberg and Marlene Dietrich in film; in architecture Walter Gropius and Mies van der Rohe.

Jazz (later to be outlawed by the Nazis as decadent) was played everywhere. Nightclubs, cabarets and cinemas sprang up all over the city, particularly in the Ku'damm area. Gender was bent, conventions shattered. The black American Josephine Baker, one of many such entertainers, stripped naked on stage every night. Nothing was impossible and nothing was forbidden – or so it seems now.

Hitler's Nazi party was advancing strongly throughout the country, though much less so in Berlin. In 1926, Joseph Göbbels was appointed to win over the city. He built up a party structure and conducted marches and rallies of the 'Brownshirts' – Stormtroopers – in predominantly working class and left wing areas of the city like Wedding. The reaction was fierce, and pitched battles in the Berlin

Treading the boards: the austere décor of Brecht's house echoes his style

streets became a daily event – but the nightmarish message of the National Socialists began to appear to many like a gleam of hope.

It was the desperation of the times that caused the Weimar government to try to use the Nazis to suppress the Bolsheviks. Following an increase in the vote for Hitler in 1930, they little by little brought the Nazis into the government. An arson attack on the Reichstag, on 28 February 1933, was Hitler's pretext to seize control. Henceforth he made his position unassailable, and became dictator of Germany.

Hitler and World War II

The first concentration camp was set up in Dachau in 1933. It received trade unionists and Jews, and anybody else whose ideology differed from that propounded by the National Socialists. This included church leaders opposed to fascism (not all were), political dissidents, homosexuals and any 'criminal element'. The writing was on the wall and the slow exodus of left wing and Jewish artists, scientists, writers and musicians from Berlin became a flood. The loss of these, and of the others who remained and were subsequently killed, impoverished the city immeasurably.

In May 1933 came the Buchverbrennung – a public burning of huge piles of books conflicting with Nazi ideology, opposite Berlin's university. Anti-Semitic attacks became so vicious and yet so frequent over several years that when, on the night of 9 November 1938, rampaging crowds of Stormtroopers in civilian clothes smashed up the majority of the city's 29 synagogues, destroyed shops and homes and attacked Jews in the street, most Berliners merely averted their eyes. This night was called 'Kristallnacht' because of the sight and sound of breaking glass.

There was opposition in Berlin, but not enough to halt the Nazis' ambitions. War was next on the agenda. Hitler proceeded with the brutal enlargement of the German state until, at last, in 1939, following his annexation of Poland, Britain and France declared war. Hitler believed the contest would be brief. At first, he seemed to be right. German troops swept through France and pushed the British off continental Europe. But in due course, the Soviet Union too was drawn into the war and then the United States. From then on, little by little, despite the impossible sacrifices he demanded from his people, Hitler's fate was sealed.

Berlin meanwhile was torn to pieces by massive Allied bombing raids. Destruction was completed during the final days of the war, in which the Fall of Berlin was the key event. Soviet troops completely encircled the

Teufelsberg, the Devil's Mountain, rose up out of war rubble

city, but it was only when the fighting reached the Reichstag that Hitler acknowledged defeat. He married his mistress, Eva Braun, and committed suicide.

Little was left in Berlin except for gaunt and burnt-out buildings and millions of tons of rubble. Uncountable lives were lost among the Russians, the German army and the civilian population. The surviving women of Berlin – there being few men left – became known as the 'Trummerfrauen' or 'rubble women', as they cleared enough debris to build a mountain in the west of the city.

Berlin Divided: Airlift and Wall

As previously arranged among the Allied leaders, administration of the city was divided between the Soviets, British, French and Americans. German forces surrendered on 8 May 1945 but the British, French and American forces did not take over the administration of their sectors from the Soviets until they arrived in the city in the early days of July. When they did, they found themselves encircled by a sea of Soviet soldiery and Soviet political control.

Free elections in the Eastern sector were quickly set aside. Nominal control was in the hands of former German Communists who had spent the war years in the Soviet Union. On the Western side, the order given by the Allies was for the gradual re-establishment of a democratic structure. As the two systems grew up in a divided nation, Germany became a theatre of conflict between the Communists and the 'Free World', with Berlin as a microcosm of the whole.

Differing ideologies made co-operation impossible, and the Soviets wanted the Allies out of West Berlin. The crunch came in June 1948 over the introduction of the Deutschmark in the Western zone and the Soviet rejection

West Berlin's air-lift lifeline is commemorated in a memorial at Tempelhof airport

of it in favour of their own system. The Berliners' vote went to the new Deutschmark. That night, the Soviets began the blockade of Berlin by switching off electricity supplies and cutting road and rail communications. The overall commander in West Berlin was General Lucius Clay. Under his inspired leadership the Allies responded by attempting to supply the whole of their sector of the city by air. At first it seemed that the city would starve, but within weeks, new runways were being built at Tempelhof and Gatow airports and a new airport was constructed at Tegel. Aircraft, loaded with supplies, were landing every 30 seconds. On 12 May 1949, the Soviet leader, Joseph Stalin, finally called off the blockade, thus tacitly admitting the Allies were in Berlin to stay. West Berliners, heavily subsidised by the Allies as a showcase for their economic system, now slowly began to prosper. The city even managed to retain its position as Germany's main industrial centre. East Berlin became the capital of a newly established German Democratic Republic (DDR).

Here matters soon went from bad to worse economically. On 16 June 1953, hearing their workloads were to be increased, construction workers marched on government headquarters. After 24 hours of a confused popular uprising, the Soviets brought out the tanks. Deaths and executions followed. Order was restored in East Berlin but it remained highly repressive. Inflamed by the prohibition of free movement and travel, lured by the material glitter of the West, great numbers of East Germans annually used West Berlin as their gateway to a new life in the West.

The response was the construction of the so-called Anti-Fascist Wall. In summer 1961 the whole of West Berlin was walled in and the citizens of the East walled out. On the western side, the Wall gradually acquired graffiti and public viewing points. On the eastern side however, the Wall was backed by a no-man's land, surveyed from sentry towers by armed soldiers. Many died trying to cross to the West.

BACKGROUND

Rathaus Schöneberg became the seat of West Berlin's government after the Blockade

Thus began one of the strangest periods in the life of the city. Under the complicated regulations for control, soldiers of four foreign armies were seen on the streets. Soviet troops came into West Berlin to change the guard at their War Memorial on Strasse des 17 Juni and took their turn in guarding Rudolf Hess, Hitler's one-time deputy and the solitary prisoner held in Spandau Prison, deep in the British sector. Spying was rife, providing the subject for such popular writers as John le Carré and Len Deighton.

John F Kennedy came to Berlin in 1963 as the young president on whose shoulders the hopes of a genuinely free world appeared to ride. His phrase, 'Ich bin ein Berliner' rang across the city and the world, to show that America would not surrender this symbolic Western bastion, however exposed it was. This was also a period when young West

Berliners began to question the ideological system under which they lived. Their protests were put down with a violence that shocked observers. In West Germany this period saw the emergence of the Red Army/Bader Meinhof terrorist faction, striking against what it saw as capitalist excess.

Meanwhile West Berlin continued to develop in its own idiosyncratic way, attracting the 'alternative' young from other states. Heavy subsidy helped the arts to flourish in both halves of the city. West Berlin acquired an avant-garde reputation. East Berlin may have seemed a little old fashioned by comparison, but theatre, opera and music flourished here as in the West.

The City United

The Wall was breached on 9 November 1989. Events had been pointing that way for some while but when it happened, it was still almost unbelievable. Nothing appeared more symbolic of a new order in Europe than crowds toasting each other in champagne by the Brandenburg Gate and surging over and through the Wall.

Earlier in 1989, the Eastern bloc states to the south of Germany had undergone anti-Soviet and generally anti-Communist revolutions. In Berlin it was an almost chance remark by a party official at a press conference which implied that citizens of East Berlin would not be stopped if they tried to enter the West. Guards at the border crossings had no warning. When joyous crowds swept down on them, they stood aside and let the people pass. It was not long before the Wall itself was being demolished.

In a period of euphoria and almost incredible optimism, Chancellor Helmut Kohl, leader of West Germany, saw that a weakened USSR had neither the will nor the wish to respond and swept on towards German reunification. Some say he carried the people with him, others that he railroaded them into unification. By 1990, Germany was one again.

Berlin entered the 1990s as the capital of reunited Germany and became the seat of government once again in June 1991, after

BACKGROUND

much debate. Sad to say, the optimism of 1990 ebbed rapidly. The first and perhaps the gravest problem was unemployment sweeping former East Germany, not excluding East Berlin. Businesses which had previously produced only to government order encountered a cut-throat competition for which they were entirely unprepared. For the tourist, there will inevitably be changes over and above the new accessibility of the whole city. The coexistence of East Berlin as a national capital and West Berlin as a free market showpiece

Looking over the city from Rathaus Schöneberg

has meant that everything, from soccer fields to museums, has been duplicated.

Undoubtedly there will be amalgamations of museums, closures of theatres and rearrangements on a grand scale. It is likely that this book, as up-to-date as possible at the time of publication, may not always have the latest details.

Over and above its problems, Berlin remains an electric, even a magnetic city, and, as always, a crucible of history. Not to see it would be to miss what may well be Europe's most fascinating capital.

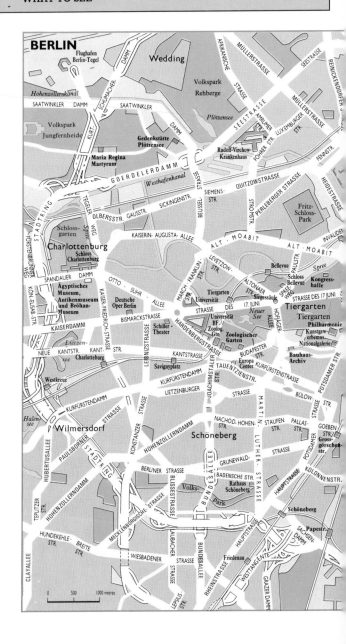

WHAT TO SEE

◆◆
ÄGYPTISCHES MUSEUM
Schlossstrasse 70, Map p 30–1
The Egyptian Museum houses only part of an outstanding collection begun in 1698 by the Elector Friedrich III. The rest now forms the splendid collection in the **Bode-Museum** in the East. The star exhibit in Charlottenburg is the head of Queen Nefertiti, sneaked out of the future Soviet sector of East Berlin in the final days of World War II.

There are other works of sculpture here, along with bronzes, papyrus, jewellery, mummy masks, vases and musical instruments from 5000BC to AD300.

Also on display is the 2,000-year-old Kalabasha Monumental Gate, presented by the Egyptian Government in recognition of German help in preserving archaeological monuments during the building of the Aswan High Dam.

Open: Monday to Thursday 9:00A.M.–5:00P.M.; Saturday and Sunday 10:00A.M.–5:00P.M.

◆◆
ALEXANDERPLATZ
Map p 44–5
Known as 'Alex', the Alexanderplatz was the focal point of old Berlin before the war and served as the centre for East Berlin during the years of Soviet domination. Famous as a meeting place, it has played a part in almost all popular revolutions, up to and including November 1989. Alexanderplatz forms a hub at the top of the grand processional way leading up via Unter den Linden from the Brandenburg Gate. But where it was once a comfortable, crowded, seedy kind of place (best described in Alfred Döblin's 1920s novel of metropolitan low life, *Berlin Alexanderplatz*, later filmed by Fassbinder), it has now become a huge and arid open space, ringed by massive Socialist architecture. The road that bounds it to the east is a full 12 lanes wide, with parking in the middle.

The single most dominant building is the Hotel Stadt Berlin, once the showpiece hotel of East Berlin but now displaced by newer rivals. More human aspects of the Alexanderplatz include ice-cream cafés and the Zille-Garten (a small garden attached to a café/restaurant and the only touch of green in Alex), the thoroughly dismal Brunnen der Völkerfreundschaft (Friendship of the Peoples Fountain), and the more cheerful World Clock, a traditional meeting-place. It tells you the time in such places as Ulan-Bator and Novosibirsk.

◆
ALTES MUSEUM
Marx-Engels-Platz, Map p 44–5
Not just the 'Old Museum', this is Berlin's oldest, but is devoted to modern East German painting. It was built by Karl Friedrich Schinkel. Within, considerable space is now devoted to exhibitions, sometimes excellent, but the paintings in the permanent

collection may soon seem to have more historical than artistic interest. Look for the powerful anti-Fascist indignation and grotesquery of Hubertus Giebe's *Widerstand*, 1953, and Volker Stelman's *Bunkerkarnaval*, 1940.

Open: Wednesday, Thursday, Saturday and Sunday 9:00A.M.–6:00P.M.; Friday 10:00A.M.–6:00P.M.

◆
ANTIKENMUSEUM
Schlossstrasse 1, Map p 30–1
Dispersed during World War II, this imperial collection of antiquities is now housed in separate museums in the East and West of the city. This one has Minoan and Mycenaean as well as Etruscan, Greek and

The classical Antikenmuseum

Roman artefacts – vases, bronzes and jewellery. The treasure of Roman silver found at Hildesheim is also displayed. The complementary exhibits of antiquities in the East are in the **Pergamon Museum**.

Open: Monday to Thursday 9:00A.M.–5:00P.M.; Saturday and Sunday 10:00A.M.–5:00P.M.

◆

BAUHAUS-ARCHIV

Klingelhöferstrasse 13, Map p 36–7

The 'Archiv' is in fact a museum, which is open most of the week. The short-lived Bauhaus has been hugely influential in the art and architecture of the 20th century – partly in stark and often box-like buildings, but also in brilliant paintings, incomparable typography, and furniture designs still in production today.

The Bauhaus was a highly original art school, where artists and craftsmen worked together in a common cause. It started up in Weimar in 1919, was driven on to Dessau when Weimar voted in a Nationalist state government, and on again to Berlin in 1929. In Berlin it came into conflict with the Nazis and was closed for good – that is, until a post-war resurrection in Chicago. The architect Walter Gropius was its first director; Mies van der Rohe was its last. Painters on the staff included Klee and Kandinsky. The work of all these is reflected in a changing display.

Open: Wednesday to Monday 11:00A.M.–5:00P.M.

◆

BERLINER DOM

Museumsinsel, Map p 44–5

This protestant cathedral and burial place of the Hohenzollern family was built at the turn of the century for Kaiser Wilhelm II. The vast High Renaissance structure of the present version seems almost shockingly ornate in contrast to the monolithic architecture by which it is surrounded. It was badly damaged during World War II and the exterior restoration work has only recently been completed.

◆◆

BERLIN-MUSEUM

Lindenstrasse 14, Map p 30–1

Formerly the Supreme Court, this grand building of 1735 was rebuilt after World War II. It charts the later centuries of Berlin's history, using models, pictures, portraits, furnished rooms, domestic artefacts and children's toys. Look for the work of Berlin's most famous cartoonist, Heinrich Zille. On the ground floor, there is an intact section of the Berlin Wall bearing classic graffiti, and a showcase of memorabilia. The same floor houses poignant exhibits of the life of the Jewish community. The museum also has a reconstruction of an old-fashioned Berlin café-bar, which is a popular place to stop for a drink or a meal. The complementary museum in the East is the **Märkisches Museum**.

Open: Tuesday to Sunday 10:00A.M.–10:00P.M.

Bode-Museum overlooks the Spree

◆◆◆
BODE-MUSEUM
Am Kupfergraben –
Monbijoubrücke, Map p 44–5
The Bode-Museum houses fine
collections of European
sculpture and a quite
astonishing display of Egyptian
antiquities (together with a fine
papyrus collection). There is
also a large and less exciting
picture gallery.
About half of the ground floor
space is taken up with
sculpture and, sometimes,
chunks of the interiors of
buildings. The Coptic
collection offers quaint stone
carving. Byzantine works
include mosaics from San
Michele in Ravenna; and there
is German medieval and,
particularly, 16th-century
polychrome wood sculpture,
full of emotion and character.
The Egyptian collection is also
on the ground floor. There are
mummies of adults and
children, the body of a two-
year-old child entirely turned
to leather, and mummified
animals, their skeletons
revealed by X-ray. Equally
haunting are the lifelike
mummy-masks, the strange
little representations of
baboons and dogs with
enormous ears.
Most of the upstairs is
occupied by paintings, worth a
look but not comparable with
the **Museen Dahlem**.
Open: Wednesday to Sunday
10:00A.M.–6:00P.M.

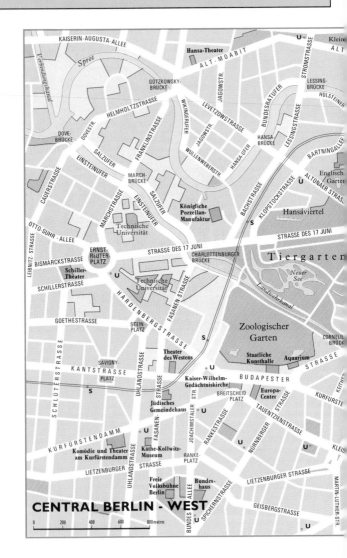

CENTRAL BERLIN - WEST

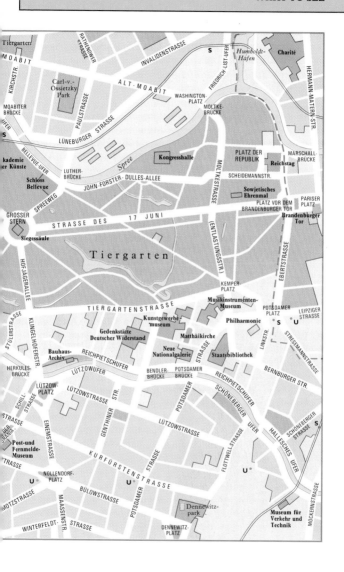

WHAT TO SEE

◆
BOTANISCHER GARTEN UND BOTANISCHES MUSEUM
Königin-Luise-Strasse 6–8, Steglitz, Map p 10–11

A colourful and pleasant place to spend a couple of hours, particularly after a session in the Dahlem museum complex near by. There are landscaped gardens, wild woods, tropical houses and greenhouses, beds of scented herbs and flowers for the blind. The Botanisches Museum is by the north entrance of the gardens, and tends to the didactic.

Open: (gardens) 9:00A.M.–8:00P.M. daily (tropical houses shut at 5:15P.M.); (museum) Tuesday to Sunday 10:00A.M.–5:00P.M.

In the Botanischer Garten

◆◆◆
BRANDENBURGER TOR
Map p 44–5

Much of the history of the city has been enacted against the backdrop of this monument. The Brandenburg Gate was built in 1791 by the neo-classical architect Carl Langhans to replace an earlier baroque toll gate, and at that time marked the western boundary of Berlin. The model was the entrance to the Acropolis in Athens, with classical columns later surmounted by the Quadriga – a four-horse chariot – driven by the goddess of peace. Though it was originally called the 'Gate of Peace', its associations have been rather the reverse. Napoleon, the victor at the battle of Jena, was so taken with the Quadriga that he sent it back to Paris in 1806. Following the fortunes of war, it was brought back a few years later. The Nazis organised torchlight processions to pass through this gate; and it was here in November 1989 that it became a symbol of joy as citizens began to tear the Wall down.

◆◆
BRECHT-HAUS
Chauseestrasse 125, Map p 44–5

The house where the great poet and playwright Bertolt Brecht spent his last years with his wife, the actress Helene Weigel, has been left largely as it was when he lived in it. Brecht abandoned Germany in 1933, finally ending up in the US. In 1948 he returned to East Berlin and set up his theatrical

Imposing Brandenburger Tor

company, the Berliner Ensemble. His library, a plain white-walled room with a pine floor, is lined with books, including detective novels, and with posters for the Berliner Ensemble. Seven different work tables are placed round the room, each for a different project. After Brecht's death, Helene Weigel lived out her years on the ground floor. The house is open for visits by a guided tour at half hour intervals.

The view from the library is over the **Dorotheenstädtischer Friedhof** (cemetery) where Brecht, Weigel and many others of Berlin's most celebrated citizens are buried, including the philosopher Georg Hegel and Karl Friedrich Schinkel, the architect.

Open: Tuesday, Wednesday and Friday 10:00A.M.–noon; Thursday 5:00–7:00P.M.; Saturday 9:30A.M.–noon and 12:30–2:00P.M.

◆◆
BRÖHAN-MUSEUM
Schlossstrasse 1a, Map p 30–1
This unexpected and pleasing museum offers Art Nouveau and Art Deco furniture, glass, ceramics, silver and so on, accompanied by many paintings and a smaller number of sculptures. Each gallery is a total room, complete with period contents from the rug on the floor to the pictures on the walls. Note especially the nudes by Willy Jaeckel and the paintings and

WHAT TO SEE

sculpture of Jean Lambert-Ducki; and do not miss the top-floor display of swirling, curvilinear Art Nouveau silver.
Open: Tuesday to Sunday 10:00A.M.–6:00P.M.

◆
BRÜCKE MUSEUM
Bussardsteig 9, Map p 10-11
The Brücke Museum is tucked away among pines and silver birches on the edge of the Grunewald in West Berlin. Die Brücke, 'the Bridge', was the name taken by a group of Expressionist artists working mainly in Dresden between 1905 and 1913. Their hallmarks were bold simplification and striking combinations of colours. The collection changes, but you should see work by Ernst Ludwig Kirchner, Karl Schmidt-Rottluff, and Emil Nolde – all still exciting today.
Open: Wednesday to Monday 11:00A.M.–5:00P.M.

◆
EHRENMAL FÜR DIE OPFER DES 20 JULI 1944
Stauffenbergstrasse 11–14, Map p 36–7
The 20 July Memorial and Gedenkstätte Deutscher Widerstand is a memorial to German resistance against fascism within the former German Army Office (easy to miss because the signs are very modest). Claus Graf Schenk von Stauffenberg, the leader of the plot to blow up Hitler on 20 July 1944 – last of several conspiracies – was chief of staff here. Wreaths stand against a wall inscribed with the names of the

Ehrenmal für die Opfer des 20 Juli

conspirators. They were shot there, illuminated by the headlights of staff cars.
The failure of the assassination attempt led to a massive round up of any possible focus of resistance to Hitler. Thousands were imprisoned, tortured and executed.
An exhibition on the second floor of the building has photographs, display notes (in German only) and contemporary documents recording the activities of the many groups within German society who refused to tolerate or ignore the outrage of National Socialism.
Open: Monday to Friday 9:00A.M.–6:00P.M.; Saturday, Sunday and holidays 9:00A.M.–1:00P.M.

◆
EPHRAIMPALAIS
Poststrasse 16, Map p 44–5
This reconstructed mansion on the border of the Nikolaiviertel, now a museum, is one of the gems of East Berlin. The original was demolished to make way for a highway, but the façade was kept safe in West Berlin, available for re-use when the area was restored. It houses a museum on Berlin, from the period of the Electors to the 19th century, with interesting paintings in particular.
Open: Monday 10:00A.M.–4:00P.M.; Tuesday and Sunday 10:00A.M.–5:00P.M.; Wednesday and Saturday 10:00A.M.–6:00P.M.

◆
EUROPA-CENTER
Map p 36–7
At the head of Tauentzienstrasse and opposite the Kaiser-Wilhelm-Gedächtniskirche, the Europa-Center is a huge shopping and office complex, with cinemas, restaurants, a casino, revue and cabaret theatre as well. Visit the Verkehrsamt (tourist information office) on the ground floor and then make your way up to the observation platform in the I-Punkt restaurant on the top floor, to get a view of the city.

The Europa-Center is an all-weather complex

WHAT TO SEE

The Breitscheidplatz, the pedestrianised area at the base of the Europa-Center, is a busy meeting place during the day – for derelicts and panhandlers as well as shoppers and sightseers. In the evening, the place is noisy with street performers and merchants, but late at night the atmosphere can become more sinister.

Fernsehturm, the ultimate TV aerial

◆
FERNSEHTURM
Alexanderplatz S-Bahn, Map p 44–5
The silhouette of the TV tower – an immense spike with a globe impaled near the top – is an inescapable element of most views of central Berlin. Depending on crowds and visibility, it is worth making the ascent to the viewing gallery (222 yards, 203m by elevator), to see Berlin spread out below. There is a revolving café on the next floor up.
Open: 9:00A.M.–midnight (last admission to viewing gallery 11:30P.M., café 11:00P.M.)
Closed: second and fourth Tuesday of each month, until 1:00P.M.

◆◆
GEDENKSTÄTTE PLÖTZENSEE
Hüttigpfad, Map p 30–1
The prison of Plötzensee, now a boys' penitentiary bordered by canals and allotments, holds one of Berlin's most powerful and depressing monuments. Visitors pass through the high walls at the side of the penitentiary to a small paved enclosure surrounded by trees. In the small, low building here, more than 2,500 people died. As well as those who resisted the dictatorship they included others merely suspected of a connection or many who were simply deemed unfit to live. Some execution proceedings were filmed and the films rushed to the Führer for his impatient inspection. Outside stands an urn containing a sample of soil from all the

concentration camps.
Open: daily, March to
September 8:00A.M.–6:00P.M.;
October and February
8:30A.M.–5:30P.M.; November
8:30A.M.–4:30P.M.; December
and January 8:30A.M.–4:00P.M.

◆

GETHSEMANES-KIRCHE
*corner of Stargarder Strasse
and Greifenhager Strasse,
Map p 30–1*
The 19th-century brick church
of Gethsemane, in Prenzlauer
Berg, became a centre of
peaceful protest in the run-up
to the events of November
1989. Slightly dank from
outside, inside a place of
sweeping balconies, it is worth
a visit as a piece of modern
history. Newspaper clippings
of the protests are pinned to a
wall within.

◆

GROSSER MÜGGELSEE
Map p 10–11
This large lake out to the east
of the city, known as the
Müggelsee, has been the main
escape for East Berliners ever
since World War II and is
traditionally crowded in
summer. Now West Berliners
have begun to use it as well.
The approach via
Friedrichshagen, with a long
straight walk down the
Bölschestrasse to the lakeside,
has a curiously mixed
atmosphere of town, country
and once-prosperous lakeside
villa territory. The workers at
the Berliner Bürger Brau
brewery, right on the water's
edge among the villas, played
a heroic, if ultimately doomed,

role in various episodes of
proletarian resistance, last
against Hitler in 1933.

◆

GRUNEWALD
Map p 10–11
The Grunewald forest on the
western reaches of the city,
bordered by the Havel River,
is a favourite recreation area
for Berliners. Much of the
forest, originally royal hunting
woods of beech and oak, was
cut down for firewood after the
war. It was replanted with
quick-growing species of birch
and ash and still is home to a
variety of wildlife including
deer and wild boar (the latter
safely enclosed).
The Avus, a pre-war motor
racing circuit converted into
an expressway, bisects the
Grunewald forest from the
Congress Centre to the
Wannsee. A grandstand
survives and some racing still
takes place here.

◆

HAUS AM CHECKPOINT
CHARLIE
*Friedrichstrasse, just off Koch
Strasse, Map p 30–1*
This is a museum dedicated to
the Wall and escapology,
situated just beside the lately
vanished Checkpoint Charlie
(the former main transit point
between East and West for
pedestrians and motorists). It
shows ingenious methods of
escape used by would-be
fugitives to the West –
balloons, tunnels, drains and
tiny vehicles with tinier secret
compartments inside them.
Open: daily 9:00A.M.–10:00P.M.

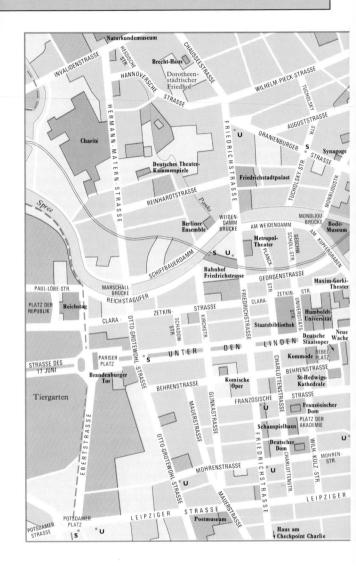

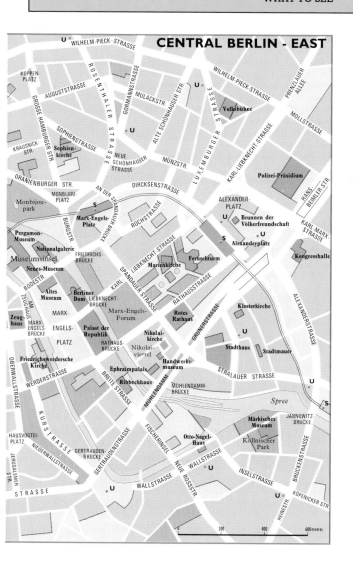

CENTRAL BERLIN - EAST

WHAT TO SEE

◆
HAVEL
Map p 10–11
Berlin is full of lakes, canals and rivers, and the Havel River forms the largest of these watery playgrounds to the west. (See **Grosser Müggelsee** for eastern lakes.) Many pleasure boat trips are available in summer. Boats on the Havel system may be joined at Spandau, Wannsee, Glienicke and other places.

◆
ICC BERLIN (INTERNATIONALES CONGRESS CENTRUM)
Messedamm, Map p 10–11
Looking like a space city or many cans of sardines, this communications and conference centre in the western outskirts opened in 1979, and symbolised the new age of Berlin as a conference city. Inside the long auditorium of the reception hall, the first impression is of red flashing lights along one side, blue on the other. Everywhere there are workers at computer stations, punching keyboards, staring into monitors. This monster communications factory houses 80 conference and meeting rooms, in some of which the tiered seating disappears at the press of a button and the conference room becomes a banquet hall. There are also restaurants, banks and shops. Guided tours are available, bookable in advance.
A quick step leads to the **Funkturm** or Radio Tower, with a high observation tower (no match for the eastern Berlin TV Tower) and a popular restaurant. The Radio and Broadcasting Museum, showing early radio technology, is at the foot of the tower.
Open: Tuesday to Saturday 10:00A.M.–6:00P.M.; Sunday 10:00A.M.–4:00P.M.

◆◆
JAGDSCHLOSS GRUNEWALD
Grunewald, Map p 10–11
This hunting lodge has been taking shape since the 16th century. Many paintings were installed here after World War II, and there is a splendid collection of Lucas Cranach the Elder.
The lodge is set on the banks of the Grunewaldsee, with cobbled courtyard, stables and a small hunting museum. On 3 November each year, St Hubert's Day (in honor of the patron of huntsmen), the exclusive riding clubs of Grunewald turn out to hunt.
Open: Tuesday to Sunday 10:00A.M.–1:00P.M.; and 1:30–6:00P.M.

◆◆
JÜDISCHES GEMEINDEHAUS
Fasanenstrasse 79–80, Map p 36–7
The synagogue where the Jewish Community House now stands was burnt down on the night of 9 November 1938 – Kristallnacht or Crystal Night, the date of a fearsome onslaught against the Jews. The new building, with only the original portal of the old synagogue still standing in front, is a place of worship and meeting, and for remembrance of the millions

Jagdschloss Grunewald

who were killed by the Nazis. It also houses an excellent kosher restaurant.

◆◆
KAISER-WILHELM-GEDÄCHTNISKIRCHE
Breitscheidplatz, by Zoo Station, Map p 36–7
Built in 1891 as a memorial to the Kaiser, this large church was bombed in 1943. It has since been left in its ruinous condition, as a reminder of the horrors of war. Today the black and jagged remains of the original, known by Berliners as the Broken Tooth, stand beside the shimmering blue reflections of stained glass from the new buildings flanking it.

WHAT TO SEE

◆◆◆
KÄTHE-KOLLWITZ-MUSEUM

Fasanenstrasse 24, Map p 36–7
Drawings, lithographs and
sculptures show the
preoccupations of Käthe
Kollwitz, a radical woman artist
who lived from 1867 to 1945.
Images of loss and despair
predominate, and include
drawings of a mother and her
dying child – all the more
poignant because they were
done before Käthe Kollwitz's
own son was killed in World
War I and her only grandson
in World War II. She resigned
from the Prussian Academy of
Art in 1933 and was forced to
stop teaching and exhibiting
by the Nazi government.
Open: Wednesday to Monday
11:00A.M.–6:00P.M.

◆
KONGRESSHALLE

*John-Foster-Dulles-Allee,
Map p 36–7*
The extraordinarily shaped
hall in the Tiergarten was a
good will gift from the United
States for the International
Building Exhibition of 1957.
The roof collapsed in 1980
causing at least one death. The
building was quickly re-
erected, contrary to the wish of
some Berliners who objected
to the pregnant oyster shape of
its roof. It is now used for
conferences, concerts and
exhibitions.

◆
KÖNIGLICHE PORZELLAN-
MANUFAKTUR

Wegelystrasse 1, Map p 36–7
Founded by Kaspar Wegely,
this porcelain manufacturing

works (KPM) received its royal
seal of approval and
trademark of the royal blue
sceptre in 1763. The
showrooms are open Monday
to Friday 9:00A.M.–6:00P.M.;
Saturday 9:00A.M.–2:00P.M.

◆◆
KÖPENICK

*S-Bahn to Köpenick Station,
then tram, bus or 20-minute
walk, Map p 10–11*
Much of the old town of
Köpenick survives, making it
potentially one of the most

Schloss Köpenick, from the park

attractive spots in Berlin and its neighbourhood. It is extremely run down, however, and is little helped by the traffic which zips round the centre. There are pleasant streets and a brick town hall with *ratskeller* (basement restaurant), and the whole area is interspersed with park, river and lake.

The main attraction is the palace, **Schloss Köpenick**. It houses the **Kunstgewerbe-museum**, part of what was once a national collection of applied art (see separate **Kunstgewerbemuseum** entry, in West Berlin).

On entry, the first pleasure is the wonderfully extravagant plaster decoration of the ceiling. The collection begins on the ground floor and is in chronological order, except for a contemporary display in the basement. Highlights include the 'treasury', with fine gold and silver from the 11th century; a panelled chamber

of 1548 from Switzerland, reassembled here; lavishly elegant 18th-century furniture; and strangely coloured Jugendstil (Art Nouveau) glass, in the hallway.
Open: Wednesday to Sunday 10:00A.M.–6:00P.M., but check for changes.

◆◆
KREUZBERG
Map p 10–11
For an overview of this old city district, climb the Hill of the Cross in Viktoriapark, which at 217 feet (66m) provides a rare high point in a generally flat city. The somewhat unattractive cross (1812–15) is by Schinkel, commemorating victories in the Napoleonic wars. Beneath is an artificial waterfall. Parts of western Kreuzberg, particularly around the handsome street of Mehringdamm, are built on the typical Berlin pattern of large outward-facing city blocks with courtyards receding within. These, as in **Prenzlauer Berg** (see separate entry) were both workplace and living quarters. The arrival of the Wall in 1961 meant that Kreuzberg was tucked away in a forgotten corner. The housing languished while intellectuals, bohemians and squatters moved in. Nowadays western Kreuzberg and its mansions are swiftly becoming gentrified, but eastern Kreuzberg retains much more of its Wall-era seediness. The most intensive squatting was on Oranienplatz. Here radical graffiti are still much in evidence, and all down Oranienstrasse there are alternative bars and restaurants. Cheap housing drew in Turkish 'guest-workers' and this part of the town has an Islamic air.

◆◆
KUNSTGEWERBEMUSEUM
Tiergartenstrasse 6,
Map p 36–7
Despite an unpromising exterior, the Museum of Applied Art is one of those West Berlin museums where a fine collection receives a brilliant display. It contains parts of the pre-World War II national collection of applied art (see **Köpenick** for the East Berlin equivalent), with some recent additions. Entry is down along the side and up a staircase to a main foyer at the back.
The collection proper starts one level below, with a fine display of crosses, stained glass, caskets and so on, from medieval to Renaissance. The sequence resumes on the top floor running from Renaissance to Art Deco. Glass and ceramics are outstanding here. The collection now carries on in the basement, coming up to date with furniture and objects of domestic use.
Open: Tuesday to Friday 9:00A.M.–5:00P.M.; Saturday and Sunday 10:00A.M.–5:00P.M.

◆◆
KURFÜRSTENDAMM
Map p 36–7
This long avenue (two miles, 3.5km), full of shops, restaurants and sidewalk cafés, street stalls and entertainers, is the heart and

main thoroughfare of modern Berlin – a position once enjoyed by the Alexanderplatz and Friedrichstrasse. Even the Möhring and Kranzler cafés were moved to the Ku'damm after World War II. Now it is close to the centre of communications, with Zoo Station, the bus terminal, Breitscheidplatz and the Europa-Center near by. It is also a classy shopping area (not just the Ku'damm itself but also the smaller adjoining streets). Many city tours begin and end here.

Originally this long road was merely the most direct route through the city to the royal hunting lodge at Grunewald forest in the west. It was considerably renovated in the 19th century with Bismarck's plans to make it a rival to the Champs Elysées in Paris.

Kurfürstendamm is a busy hunting ground for the city's shoppers

WHAT TO SEE

◆ LÜBARS

Map p 10–11

On the northern edge of West Berlin, Lübars is a surprisingly rural spot to find within the city limits. With cobbled country roads and riding stables, a pair of pubs, an old-fashioned village church and the oldest house in Berlin, it remains an agreeable retreat for a summer afternoon.

◆ MARIA REGINA MARTYRUM

Heckerdamm 230–2,
Map p 30–1

This stark and sombre Catholic church was built in 1963 as a memorial to the 'martyrs to freedom of faith and conscience in the years 1933–1945'. Heavily symbolic, it was built to face in the direction of Plötzensee prison, scene of the execution of many resistance workers (see **Gedenkstätte Plötzensee**). The open space in front of the church is surrounded by high walls of basalt slabs to create the impression of a concentration camp yard. In the crypt there is a most moving bronze *Pieta* by Fritz König, and a gravestone provides a symbolic resting place for those executed at Plötzensee. The church is plain to the point of austerity, with simple wooden benches, a large abstract mural by Georg Meistermann, and a tiny 14th-century Gothic Madonna and Child. Natural light filters through from concealed windows.

Open: daily 9:00A.M.–5:30P.M.

◆◆ MARIENKIRCHE

Karl-Liebknecht-Strasse 8,
Map p 44–5

Once tightly packed among surrounding houses but now in open space across from the Rotes Rathaus (Red Town Hall), the Marienkirche is a Gothic survivor of World War II right in the city centre. Built in 1262, rebuilt at the end of the 14th century and needing not much more than new windows after World War II, it is open and spacious inside, with an ornate baroque pulpit by Andreas Schlüter and plenty of elaborate memorials to the departed. A medieval wall painting rediscovered in 1860 and now badly faded by pollution shows a 'Dance of Death', inspired by an outbreak of the plague in 1484.

◆◆ MÄRKISCHES MUSEUM

Am Köllnischer Park,
Map p 44–5

This imposing fake Gothic building was founded in 1874 by the City of Berlin, and houses a city museum. There is a collection of fine glass and porcelain, earthenware and wrought ironwork, and theatrical memorabilia from the great days of Max Reinhardt. Paintings of Berlin show the city's classical buildings taking shape, and there are romantic studies of a rural Kreuzberg, with more recent Berlin street scenes by Lesser Ury. Outside, a statue of Heinrich Zille shows Berlin's best-loved cartoonist sketching while a local lad peers over his

Märkisches Museum and Zille statue

shoulder. A couple of Berlin bears are kept in the small Köllnischer Park immediately behind the museum.
Open: Wednesday to Friday 9:00A.M.–5:00P.M.; Saturday 9:00A.M.–6:00P.M.; Sunday 10:00A.M.–6:00P.M.

◆◆
MARTIN-GROPIUS-BAU
*Stresemannstrasse 110,
Map p 30–1*
This lavish 19th-century building, one of the most

spectacular in Berlin, houses a notable collection of Berlin art, and material on Jewish history. Until the events of 1989, the Wall pressed so close up to its front door that a main entrance was established in the back. Across the road from it in East Berlin there stands the former Prussian parliament, and next door again the former Nazi Air Ministry, grim and grey. Next door to the Gropius-Bau itself

WHAT TO SEE

Ornate Martin-Gropius-Bau

stood Prinz Albrechtstrasse 8, the Gestapo headquarters, also used as a postal address for those incarcerated in concentration camps. It was one of a row of buildings obliterated after World War II in an attempt to purge hateful memories. Part of the cellars of the headquarters is now occupied by the **Topography of Terror Museum**, showing photographs and text about the people held there. (*Open*: 10:00A.M.–6:00P.M.)

Inside Martin-Gropius-Bau, the two-storeyed central space with columns in black and gold is one of Berlin's leading exhibition spaces. The paintings and sculptures of the permanent collection run from the late 19th century, through Expressionism, Dada and Constructivism into the Neue Sachlichkeit (New Objectivity) which followed, then on again through World War II and up into the 1980s. The range is very wide, from Lesser Ury street scenes to brilliant constructions by Naum Gabo. The Jewish exhibition is concerned mainly with documenting the human and cultural importance of the Jewish community. Much of the display is in written format, in German only.

Open: Tuesday to Sunday 10:00A.M.–6:00P.M. (sometimes later in summer).

◆◆◆ MUSEEN DAHLEM

Zehlendorf, Map p 10–11
The leafy suburbs of southwest
Berlin are the setting for this
prestigious museum complex,
set up as an alternative to the
then Communist Humboldt
University in East Berlin in
1948 and largely funded at its
inception by the Henry Ford
Foundation.

It is best to plan your route
fairly carefully because each
outstanding collection seems to
run into another. Pick up a
Wegweiser (plan) from the
information desk.

The **Museum für Völkerkunde**
(Ethnography Museum) covers
Ancient America, including
Peruvian pottery and
Guatemalan sculpture; Africa,
including Benin bronzes; the
South Seas, including boats
and houses; and Asia,
including Tang ceramics and
Indonesian masks and
puppets. Displays change
regularly.

For many the **Gemäldegalerie**
(Picture Gallery) is the high
point of Dahlem.

The Italian rooms are
marvellous, though not unique,
with works by masters from
Botticelli to Titian and
Caravaggio. German painting
is good in parts, with Cranach
the Elder and Hans Holbein
both featured. There is fine
Spanish work from Velázquez,
Zurbarán and Goya, and a
strong display from the English
and Scottish 18th century. But
the area in which Dahlem may
be the best in the world is in
early Netherlandish paintings,
the so-called Flemish primitives.

Room 143 offers three Van
Eycks including the gemlike
Madonna in the Church. Petrus
Christi, a contemporary, offers
St Barbara and the strange
portrait of a *Young Woman*,
her eyes like candle-flames
laid sideways. Rogier van der
Weyden, considered by some
as great a master as Van Eyck,
is almost entirely responsible
for Room 144. The collection
continues, with treasures like
Ouwater's *Raising of Lazarus*,
Bosch's *John on Patmos*, and
Bruegel's *Netherlandish
Proverbs.* Beyond this section
is a notable choice of Dutch
works by Vermeer and
contemporaries, and a
magnificent gathering of
Rembrandts.

Museen Dahlem is a treasure-house

WHAT TO SEE

The **Skulpturengalerie** (Sculpture Gallery) ranges from early Christian German Gothic and Italian Renaissance sculpture, in bronze, ivories, gold and wood. There is also a display of miniatures from the 16th to 18th centuries.

The museums of **Indian, Islamic and East Asian art** offer a wonderful display of the most beautiful art and artefacts – pictures, wall hangings, sculptures, carpets and tiles, individually lit against a black background.

This is a museum to come back to again and again. It also has a separate children's section, and a Museum for the Blind.

Open: Tuesday to Sunday 10:00A.M.–5:00P.M.

◆

MUSEUM FÜR DEUTSCHE VOLKSKUNDE

Im Winkel 6, Map p 10–11
Five minutes' walk from the main Dahlem museums, this is a place to see the popular, mostly rural, culture of the German-speaking peoples of central Europe. There are some beautifully decorated chests and cradles, and folk costumes, domestic tools and craftwork from Swiss and Austrian as well as German sources.

Open: Tuesday to Friday 9:00A.M.–5:00P.M.; Saturday and Sunday 10:00A.M.–5:00P.M.

◆◆

MUSEUM FÜR VERKEHR UND TECHNIK

Trebinner Strasse 9, Map p 36–7
An entertaining jumble of a museum on the theme of transportation and technology. Displays include huge stuffed oxen pulling a cart, light Fokker aircraft suspended from the ceiling, cars, buses and motorbikes and, in the old workshops of the Anhalter Bahnhof, a great collection of early trains. The technology is represented by ancient domestic appliances, early typewriters, and modern computers, paper presses and weaving looms. Anything that can withstand the curious touch of young children is available for hands-on treatment, an attraction for adults, too.

Open: Tuesday and Wednesday 9:00A.M.–5:50P.M.; Thursday and Friday 9:00A.M.–9:00P.M.; Saturday and Sunday 10:00A.M.–6:00P.M.

◆◆

MUSIKINSTRUMENTEN-MUSEUM

Tiergartenstrasse 1, Map p 36–7
A light and cheerful museum on two floors, it houses a collection of musical instruments from the 16th century to the present day, including ancient bagpipes and the latest electronic instruments. The exhibition continues downstairs in the basement where there is a café-bar and a small stage. It is a bonus if your visit coincides with a demonstration of a particular instrument, but there are special tours on Saturday mornings at 11:00, free for children.

Open: Tuesday to Friday 9:00A.M.–5:00P.M.; Saturday and Sunday 10:00A.M.–5:00P.M.

◆◆◆
NATIONALGALERIE
Museumsinsel, Map p 44–5
The setting is one of the great mock-classical buildings of Museumsinsel, in this case a vast, pollution-blackened Corinthian temple of 1866–76, built originally for state receptions. Modern visitors duck in by a door below. Inside the show is stolen by the brilliant colours of the early 20th-century German Expressionists, in the central gallery.

Elsewhere, some of the most interesting paintings are the ones concerned with Berlin. Look out for Menzel's charming studies of Frederick the Great at Potsdam; and the paintings of military parades on Unter den Linden, by Franz Krüger (1797–1857). These are countered by a huge Menzel scene of the interior of a Berlin steelworks. Note also Walter Leistikow's romantically gloomy view of the Grunewaldsee (1895), a range of works by Lesser Ury, and a bright Kokoschka of the Brandenburg Gate and Pariser Platz (1926). Impressionists, Post-Impressionists and Fauves are represented in the collection as well.

Open: Wednesday, Thursday, Saturday and Sunday 9:00A.M.–6:00P.M.; Friday 10:00A.M.–6:00P.M.

The old Nationalgalerie

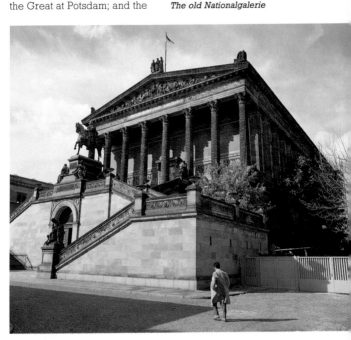

◆◆◆
NEUE NATIONALGALERIE
Potsdamer Strasse 50,
Map p 36–7

Mies van der Rohe designed this airy pavilion in glass and steel (built 1965–8). It was his last commission for a city from which he was exiled for many years, and forms part of West Berlin's Cultural Complex running south from the Potsdamer Platz end of the Tiergarten. It includes the **Kunstgewerbemuseum**, **Musikinstrumenten-Museum**, and **Staatsbibliothek** (see separate entries), and the Philharmonie concert hall. The Neue Nationalgalerie contains a wide range of works of major schools, including German Romantics and Realists, French and German Impressionists, Expressionists, Bauhaus and Surrealists. One of the first encountered is Adolph von Menzel's much-loved painting of *Frederick the Great's Flute Concert at Potsdam*, with the old man playing away under the chandeliers. The German Expressionists should not be

Outside the Neue Nationalgalerie

days when it was known as the 'Diplomat's Church' and served the embassies on this edge of the Tiergarten.
Open: Tuesday to Friday 9:00A.M.–5:00P.M.; Saturday and Sunday 10:00A.M.–5:00P.M.

◆◆
NEUE WACHE
Unter den Linden, Map p 44–5
Schinkel's New Guard House, with more than a touch of the Greek temple, appears in many 19th-century paintings, with soldiers lounging elegantly against its Doric columns. After World War II, it was decided to make the Neue Wache a monument to anti-militarism and anti-Fascism. A perpetual flame burns beside the grave of the unknown soldier and the unknown resistance fighter.

◆
NIKOLAIKIRCHE
Nikolaiviertel, Map p 44–5
This twin-towered church stands at the heart of the Nikolaiviertel district, which is named after the church. Some of the lower level is original but most of the remainder, lofty as it is, is reconstructed. The church houses an extension of the **Märkisches Museum** (separate entry), with models showing the development of Berlin and Neu-Kölln as medieval river settlements. It also has medieval artefacts and sculptures, and a great many florid baroque memorials. Outside, there is a fountain with the Berlin bear.
Open: Wednesday to Sunday 9:00A.M.–5:00P.M.

missed, and there are intriguing sculptural artefacts by Hans Arp (1887–1966) and Kurt Schwitters (1887–1948). But the most powerful picture must be *Stützen der Gesellschaft* (Pillars of Society) by George Grosz (1893–1959), painted in 1926. One of the most horrible of the ferocious figures shown is wearing a swastika.
From the Nationalgalerie you can see the sad old church of Matthäikirche, set in a waste land far removed from the

WHAT TO SEE

◆◆
NIKOLAIVIERTEL
Map p 44–5
The Nikolaikirche (page 59) is the centre of this entirely rebuilt area. It lies between the Rotes Rathaus and the Spree, and is small but very successful, providing interesting streets to wander in, pubs, restaurants, a good museum (the **Ephraimpalais**, see separate entry) and more atmosphere than might be anticipated.

Nikolaiviertel, where modern architecture recalls pre-war style

◆◆
OLYMPIASTADION
Map p 10–11.
The 'Reich sport centre' was
built for the 11th summer
Olympics (1936) by Werner
March. This was an occasion to
show the world the
achievements of the chief city
of Nazi Germany. But when the
black athlete Jesse Owens won
four gold medals, denting the
notion of Aryan superiority,
Hitler left his place on the
podium in disgust. The stadium
is still used for all sorts of
sporting events. For the best
overall view of the stadium and
the Grunewald forest go up the
bell tower. An elevator runs to
the top from April to October.

◆◆
OTTO-NAGEL-HAUS
Märkisches Ufer, Map p 44–5
This small museum-gallery is in
one of the well-restored 18th-
century mansions on the
Märkisches Ufer, in the heart
of East Berlin. Many of the
works are by Otto Nagel
(1894–1967) who became much
admired by the GDR. In the
1920s he was painting dark
grey, powerfully miserable
scenes of proletarian life. By
the early 1940s, despite the
war, his palette had lightened
and his Berlin street scenes
became actually pretty. There
is also outstanding small-scale
sculpture by Käthe Kollwitz
and Theo Balden. Painters to
note include the sardonically
watchful Hans Grundig
(1901–58) and Conrad
Felixmuller (1897–1977).
Open: Sunday to Thursday
10:00A.M.–6:00P.M.

◆◆◆
PERGAMON-MUSEUM
Museumsinsel, Map p. 44–5
Traditionally the most
prestigious museum in Berlin,
the Pergamon is the fruit of
imperial purchase and plunder
on an epic scale. It contains at
least two of the most
remarkable buildings of the
ancient world, and is a
marvellous but foot-wearying
place. If possible, it is best to
make several short visits.
The **architectural display** is on
the ground floor. First on entry
is the altar from the ancient
Greek and Roman city of
Pergamon (now in Turkey),
round which the whole
museum is built. It is vast, with
the widest of marble stairways
ascending towards a low but
very wide pillared portal. All
round the base (and the rest of
the gallery) run huge sculpted
friezes.
To the left there is a Hellenistic
room, with more from
Pergamon and immense
columns from elsewhere. In a
gallery to the right is the
astoundingly elaborate – and
beautiful – Roman gateway to
the market at Miletus. Pass
through this room to the right
and you will encounter an
even greater surprise – the
whole of the Ishtar Gate of
Babylon, built during the reign
of Nebuchadnezzar II
(604–562BC). Stretching away
from the gate runs the
processional way of Ancient
Babylon, full of tooth-gnashing
lions. This is the heart of the
West Asiatic collection.
The **East Asian collection** is on
the top floor in the wing to the

left as you face the building. Among other things, it takes the visitor on a chronological tour of Chinese porcelain. Architecture apart, the major element of the **Greek and Roman antiquities** is sculpture, running from archaic through classical Greek to Roman, and ending with carved tombs and urns of the greatest beauty and elaboration.

Upstairs is the **Islamic collection** which some think the finest of them all. It includes not merely the extraordinary carved façade of the castle of Mshatta in Jordan but also a huge range of smaller artefacts – carpets, glass and wooden inlays, tiled

Pergamon-Museum's stern façade

prayer-niches from mosques, an amazing panelled room from a private house in Aleppo, Indian miniatures and so on through a range of treasures. The **Ethnography Museum** is different in scale, style and intent. Hidden away in the basement under Greek and Roman sculpture, a small gallery shows arts and crafts with some nice objects in wood particularly, and then moves on, via an anti-Fascist section on the Jews, to a display of Berlin costume.

Open: daily 9:00A.M.–6:00P.M. (Friday 10:00A.M.–6:00P.M.). Only parts of the museum are open on Monday and Tuesday. These include the major architectural exhibits on the ground floor.

◆◆
PFAUENINSEL

'Peacock Island' is a nature reserve linked to the Glienicke Park/Berliner Forest by a regular ferry service across the Havel. It was used by Friedrich Wilhelm II as a romantic hideaway for himself and his mistress, Countess Wilhelmine von Lichtenau. Here he built a mock ruin, the Schloss Pfaueninsel – of limited interest except for the existence (rare for Berlin) of the original furniture and decoration, wallpapers, paintings and bathrooms. The island was filled with exotic creatures,but only peacocks remained by 1842. Now, it is a popular picnic spot for Berliners. This is a 'no smoking, no dogs and no music' island.

*The Berliner Schauspielhaus,
centrepiece of Platz der Akademie*

◆◆◆
PLATZ DER AKADEMIE
Map p 44–5
Until its almost total obliteration
in 1944, this vast square was
regarded as one of the great
showpieces of Europe. Now,
with restoration nearing
completion, it is claimed as a
great example of the post-war
resurrection of East Berlin,
with its two cathedrals forming
a kind of grand entrance way
to the Berliner Schauspielhaus
(theatre). It is sometimes
known by its old name of
Gendarmenmarkt.
The earliest of the three main
buildings was the Französicher
Dom or French Cathedral. It
was begun in 1701 for the
Huguenots invited to Berlin 16
years before by the Great
Elector. Today, there is a small
museum of Huguenot history in
the base of the tower, with the
'Turmstube' or Tower Inn at
about fourth-floor level. Climb

up further for the gallery
offering fine views of the Platz
der Akademie and of a wide
horizon.
On the far side of the square,
the Deutscher Dom (German
Cathedral) served the
Lutheran community. It was
almost contemporary with the
French and has a matching
tower (both towers were built
by Frederick the Great in the
late 1700s).
The theatre between the
churches was designed by
Schinkel and is one of his finest
buildings.

◆◆
POTSDAMER PLATZ
Map p 44–5
It is said that more traffic passed
through the Potsdamer Platz in
the 1920s and 1930s than
through any other city square

WHAT TO SEE

in Europe. Berlin's first traffic light was here. After World War II, and particularly after the Wall came running through in 1961, it became famous instead for its ghostly emptiness. Today the traffic goes bowling through again, but the Potsdamer Platz is still very odd. Those on foot may cross the devastation to stroll on the site of Hitler's Chancery and up on to the little mound beyond. It marks the site of the bunker where he killed himself.

The line of the Wall can be followed north to the Brandenburg Gate; or walk south to the popular, populous and rather murky Sunday morning market held on the Reichpietschufer.

◆◆
PRENZLAUER BERG
Map p 30–1
Prenzlauer Berg, particularly the part lying just east of Schönhauser Allee, has more to offer than any other district of East Berlin except for Mitte and possibly Köpenick. It was a teeming 19th-century residential and manufacturing district, built on the typical Berlin pattern of imposing façades giving way to a series of courtyards. Though still in general very run down, with balconies ready to drop like stones on the heads of passers by, its potential is revealed by the streets that have been done up, revealing the original façades. A Käthe Kollwitz bronze of herself in the square named after her, watches over the children of the district where she lived.

◆◆
RATHAUS SCHÖNEBERG
Martin-Luther-Strasse,
Map p 30–1
Schöneberg Town Hall was the seat of government for West Berlin after 1948. From its balcony, President John F Kennedy made his speech of support for the people of West Berlin in 1963. His words 'Ich bin ein Berliner' – 'I am a Berliner' – created only momentary confusion among those for whom the word Berliner means 'jelly doughnut' as well as 'native of the city'. The bell that rings at noon each day from the top of the tower is a copy of the Liberty Bell in Philadelphia, donated by the United States in 1950.

The battle-scarred Reichstag

◆◆◆
REICHSTAG
Platz der Republik,
Map p 36–7
No building in Berlin evokes the drama of recent German history more clearly than the German Parliament. It was built in 1884–94 from war reparations exacted from the French after the Franco-Prussian war; the new Republic was announced from its balcony in 1918; and it was the burning of the Reichstag in 1933 which provided the excuse for Hitler's unchallenged assumption of dictatorial powers. In the last days of the Reich, these rooms and corridors were the scene for the final battle between Soviet forces and the defending SS troops.
Now restored apart from its original dome and the profuse marks of shell-fire, the Reichstag houses the permanent exhibition, 'Fragen an die Deutsche Geschichte' – 'Questions on German history', from 1800 to the present day. Themes include National Socialism and later issues like the rise of terrorist groups from the 1960s.
Near the back of the building, crosses on the embankment of the River Spree are a memorial to those who died as they tried to cross the river to escape to the West.

◆
ROTES RATHAUS
Alexanderplatz, Map p 44–5
After a spell as town hall of East Berlin alone, this splendid brick building has been restored as the seat of the mayor of a unified Berlin. Built in 1861–9 and rebuilt after the war, it is decorated with the so-called 'Berlin Chronicle' – a terracotta frieze.

◆
SCHLOSS BELLEVUE
Spreeweg, Map p 36–7
This summer palace in Tiergarten was originally built for the younger brother of Frederick the Great in 1785. It was completely rebuilt after World War II. Now it is the official Berlin residence of the President of the Federal Republic of Germany. Guided tours can be arranged in advance. The house is open to the public when the President is not at home, but the gardens are open to visitors until sunset each day.

WHAT TO SEE

◆◆
SCHLOSS CHARLOTTENBURG

Luisenplatz, Map p 30–1
Schloss Charlottenburg, the one major Prussian palace still to be seen in the city, was built as a small summer palace for the future Queen Sophie Charlotte in 1695, in what was then a rural retreat. It was later enlarged, and now offers three main areas to visit. These are the Royal Apartments; the Knobelsdorff Wing (with more royal rooms, plus pictures); and the palace park (with three smaller buildings to see). For tours (in German) of the **Royal Apartments**, cross the courtyard by Andreas Schlüter's much admired equestrian statue of the Great Elector, and enter to the left of the main door. Visitors are led through increasingly grand baroque rooms built in imitation of the French royal style. The finest is the Ovale Saal, with tall windows, gilt and carving. The Porzellankabinett (porcelain room) reveals a taste for chinoiserie gone mad, and the chapel has a painted ceiling portraying the Virgin, looking like Sophie Charlotte. The **Knobelsdorff Wing** has rooms containing paintings from the National Gallery's Romantic collection. On the right you will find the hyper-real, hyper-romantic pictures of Caspar David Friedrich (1774–1840), depicting everything from mauve mist on mountain tops to solitary figures brooding by storm-swept seas. There are also powerful works by the Berlin architect Karl Friedrich

Schinkel. Some show vast, fantastical Gothic churches, others are drawn from Ancient Greece. Other ground-floor rooms show 19th-century palace décor and furniture, portraits, and Berlin cityscapes.
Up on the first floor, blinding in its new gilt, is the reconstructed **Golden Gallery**, built for Frederick the Great. His apartments at the far end of the Knobelsdorff Wing

Once-rural Schloss Charlottenburg

contain a number of Watteau paintings.

Immediately behind the palace is a formal, baroque garden, surrounded by the informal **palace park**. There are three buildings in the park which all deserve a visit. The **Schinkel Pavilion** is charming inside. It was built in 1825 as a summerhouse for Friedrich Wilhelm III, and stands just round the far corner of the Knobelsdorff Wing.

Downstairs, note the set of green KPM (Royal Porcelain Factory) china, with Iron Cross; upstairs, the paintings stand out, with another Gothic cathedral fantasy by Schinkel. (*Open*: Tuesday to Sunday 10:00A.M.–5:00P.M.)

Pretty in pale green, with white columns and dome, the **Belvedere** lies further back in the park and close to the

WHAT TO SEE

China in the Belvedere

canal. Once used for taking tea, it is now a porcelain museum (*open*: as Schinkel Pavilion).

The small Doric temple on the west side of the park is the **Mausoleum**. It was completed in the early 19th century for Queen Luise, wife of Friedrich Wilhelm III who was also buried here. Princes, kaisers and their spouses followed till the end of the century. (*Open*: as Schinkel Pavilion, April to October only.)

Open: Tuesday to Sunday 10:00A.M.–5:00P.M., with later opening hours operating in summer.

◆◆
SCHLOSS GLIENICKE
Wannsee, Map p 10–11

The painter and architect Karl Friedrich Schinkel built this little Italianate pleasure palace in 1826. The palace itself is closed to the public, but the gardens are open and form one of the prettiest corners of Berlin. The front of the palace faces on to the main Berlin-Potsdam road at the Glienicker Brücke (bridge), former border point between East and West and site of dramatic spy exchanges. The back of the palace looks out past columns, pavilions and huge beech trees, to open lake and sky, with the fake ruins of Frederick the Great's Sanssouci beyond. Fragments of romantic stonework from elsewhere are built into the courtyard walls at the rear of the main building, and there is a particularly pretty rotunda overlooking the bridge.

The **Volkspark Klein-Glienicke** is a landscaped park running back from Glienicke Palace towards the **Pfaueninsel** (see separate entry). Berliners flock here on summer weekends, filling the parking lots. There is a lakeside trail through woods to the small Russian church of Nikolskoe, complete with onion dome. This was built for Tsar Nikolas of Russia by his father-in-law, Friedrich Wilhelm III. Russian-style log-cabin restaurants serve meals, and the ferry point to the Pfaueninsel is within easy walking distance. Boats depart from Glienicke to all main destinations on the lakes.

◆◆◆
SIEGESSÄULE
Strasse des 17 Juni, Map p 30–1
The Victory Column stands in the 'Grosser Stern' (Great Star) Square in Strasse des 17 Juni. Perched at a height of 220 feet (67m) the golden winged creature on top, holding aloft a victory garland, is a landmark for miles around. The column commemorates successful wars against Denmark, Austria and France, and is adorned with the barrels of captured cannons. Mosaics at the base celebrate the achievement of German unity. Others (now removed) showed military conquests. Climb the spiral staircase for fine city views. Strasse des 17 Juni is named after the terrible day of 17 June 1953, when Russian tanks crushed an uprising in East Berlin.

Open: Easter to October, Tuesday to Sunday 9:00A.M.–6:00P.M.; Monday 1:00–6:00P.M.

Siegessäule, an eye-catching sight

◆◆
SOWJETISCHES EHRENMAL
Strasse des 17 Juni, Map p 36–7
The heroic bronze of a Soviet soldier in greatcoat and helmet stands as a memorial to the many thousands of Soviets soldiers who died in the battle for Berlin in the last days of the war. The two tanks flanking him were among the first to reach the city in 1945; the

The massive Sowjetisches Ehrenmal

surrounding marble was taken from Hitler's headquarters. The Soviet Memorial stands within former West Berlin, but was guarded until reunification by young Soviet soldiers. A few yards away, the statue of Der Rufer – the Caller – faces east and calls for peace.

◆
SPANDAU
Map p 10–11
The moated citadel at Spandau and the Old Town at the confluence of the rivers Spree and Havel make a pleasant out-of-centre visit. Spandau Prison, however, which for many years contained Hitler's deputy Rudolf Hess as its sole inmate, was obliterated after his death in 1987.

The 16th-century **Zitadelle**, handsome in reddish brick, stands on the site of an early castle. It protected Berlin from the northwest and acted as a checkpoint for river access. Crossing the moat, visitors enter by an impressive gateway, with a black imperial eagle. Above the main gateway is a museum with war machinery and other curiosities from the Middle Ages. The oldest part of the fortress is the crenellated Juliusturm, or Julius Tower (strictly for the energetic). This gives fine views of fortress, river and moat; other landmarks are the BMW motorcycle factory, and two power stations, one very modern, the other built entirely from components brought in during the Berlin Airlift.
Open: Tuesday to Friday

Spandau's citadel across the moat

9:00A.M.–5:00P.M.; Saturday and Sunday 10:00A.M.–5:00P.M. Though largely reconstructed, Spandau **Old Town** is made agreeable by its pedestrian precinct, tall brick church and a number of half-timbered buildings, some of them genuine survivors. Take a stroll – and a creamy cake in the *Konditorei* opposite the Nikolaikirche.

◆
STAATSBIBLIOTHEK
Potsdamer Strasse 33,
Map p 36–7
Designed by Hans Scharoun, along with the Philharmonie across the road, this is one of the most modern and best-stocked libraries in Europe, open to all and much used by students. Make your way

through the bicycle racks outside into the front hall, where you will find help on how to use the library. Racks of major European and American newspapers provide an easy way of keeping up to date.
Open: Monday to Friday 9:00A.M.–9:00P.M.; Saturday 9:00A.M.–5:00P.M.

◆
TEMPELHOF LUFTBRÜCKENDENKMAL
Tempelhof, Map p 30–1
The Airlift Memorial consists of three arcs shooting westwards into the sky at the entrance to Tempelhof airport. They symbolise the three air corridors which kept the city supplied with essentials during

WHAT TO SEE

the Berlin Blockade of 1948/9 – including all the material required to build Spandau power station. The memorial is dedicated to the 77 airmen and groundcrew who died in crashes attempting to land.

◆
TEUFELSBERG
Map p 10–11
After World War II, the bombed ruins of the city were heaped together in mounds by the *Trummerfrauen*, or 'rubble women' (there being few men left to do anything) and transferred to a huge heap in the west of the city. The heap grew into a mountain in the hilly, forested terrain just south of the Olympic stadium, and acquired the name Teufelsberg or Devil's Mountain. Here, Berliners come to fly their kites and in the winter, to ski and toboggan. The summit of the mountain is out of bounds to all but US army personnel.

◆◆
TIERGARTEN
Map p 36–7
Tiergarten, the wooded parkland in the middle of Berlin, literally means 'animal garden'. Until the beginning of the 18th century it was a hunting reserve of wild boar and deer for the use of the Electors. It was devastated in World War II, but has been tidied and replanted, and is once again becoming an important recreation area for Berliners. The most pleasant area for walking is along the canal banks and round the Neuer See behind the Zoo.

◆◆
TREPTOWER PARK SOWJETISCHES EHRENMAL
Map p 36–7
Five thousand Soviet soldiers, killed in the last days of the Battle of Berlin in 1945, are buried in the memorial ground of this park. The statue of a grieving mother stands at one end of a long avenue, and a monumental sculpture of a Soviet soldier at the other. In a chamber below, mosaics depict grieving Soviet citizenry among a profusion of flowers. Wedding couples came here to pay their respects, often leaving a bright scatter of carnations before the statue of the grieving mother.

◆◆◆
UNTER DEN LINDEN AND MUSEUMSINSEL

Map p 44–5

Unter den Linden is the processional way from the Brandenburg Gate to Museumsinsel on the Spree, knocked about by time and World War II, with some horrendous building from the 1960s and quantities of quite brilliant reconstruction. It is well worth walking the whole of it. Starting at the Brandenburg Gate (see **Brandenburger Tor**), you first arrive at Pariser Platz (Paris Square). Before the Wall came down, the Pariser Platz was out of bounds. Now there is a thriving Sunday morning market, with Soviet uniforms, *schnell imbiss* (fast food) stalls and hurdy-gurdy organs mounted on stroller wheels. Next, on either side of the start of Unter den Linden, there come large, dreary buildings in glass and pale green plastic, containing what were until recently embassies and East German ministries. The avenue itself is 200 feet (61m) across, replanted with four rows of fragrant if still quite spindly linden trees.

On the right is the enormous Soviet embassy, with a staring white bust of Lenin in front and

Crossing the Spree, from Unter den Linden to Museumsinsel

Under the lime trees

statues of heroic workers on the roof. This is followed by the Soviet Trade Delegation, Intourist and Aeroflot.

In the next block, still to the right, the **Komische Oper**, or Comic Opera, has its offices (the theatre is behind). There is a shop selling art books and music followed immediately by a showroom for Meissen porcelain.

Friedrichstrasse now crosses Unter den Linden. It is hard to imagine the cafés, restaurants, luxury hotels and shops which once lined this part of Unter den Linden, and hard to remember that it was at the corner of Friedrichstrasse that first a whistle and then a trumpet were used to control the incredible volume of traffic at the start of the century. The **Grand Hotel**, Berlin's classiest accommodation, stands on the right.

After just one more block, the grand old buildings of Prussian history begin, some battle scarred, others entirely rebuilt, many very recently. Some are full of the heavy, militaristic aspiration of the 1890s and 1900s. Others reach back into a more graceful age, though almost all are rather stark. First building in the grander sequence is on the left, the **Staatsbibliothek** (National Library) (1903–14). Dark and threatening on a winter evening, its many bullet holes have been patched with lighter-coloured stone. Next on the left comes **Humboldt University**. Designed by Knobelsdorff, it was originally the palace of Frederick the Great's younger brother. Statues and urns along the skyline are a dominant feature of the whole of this part of the street. In front of the university, two statues represent the brilliant Humboldt brothers, the naturalist and explorer Alexander, and Wilhelm, who founded the university. Frederick the Great, in tricorn hat, sits astride his horse in the middle of the road. The wide open space is the **Bebelplatz** (its modern name celebrates a 19th-century Socialist activist), once the Opernplatz, scene of the Nazi book-burning in May 1933. The big building beside it is called the **Kommode** or Chest of Drawers, because of the inverse curve of its handsome façade. Down at the far end of the Bebelplatz is **St Hedwig's Cathedral**, a pleasing little structure with an outsize dome. Back on the corner of Unter den Linden, more or less in front of Frederick, is the **Deutsche**

Staatsoper (State Opera) commissioned by Frederick and designed by Knobelsdorff. Still on the righthand side, beyond the opera house and after an open space with grass and trees, comes the **Operncafé**, originally part of a string of palaces. This and the stark, white Foreign Ministry of the former GDR, bring the righthand side of Unter den Linden to an end. The real climax comes on the left: see separate entries for the **Neue Wache** and the **Zeughaus**, the finest building on Unter den Linden.

Museumsinsel is reached from Unter den Linden by a bridge with three Schinkel statues to either side. To your left is an open space with trees (the former Lustgarten), with the **Berliner Dom**, the city's main cathedral, on the far side (see separate entry). Behind the Lustgarten to the left are crammed the majority of Berlin's great museums (always excluding the Dahlem complex in the West). See separate entries for the **Altes Museum**, the **Nationalgalerie**, the **Pergamon** and **Bode-Museum**; also here is the Neues-Museum, still in ruins. To the right of the bridge, the scene consists mainly of an enormous, barren square, which, together with the former Lustgarten, comprises the Marx-Engels-Platz. The huge building in copper-coloured glass confronting the Dom is the Palast der Republik (the Dom's reflection is a favourite photo opportunity). East Germany was ruled from here

WHAT TO SEE

until its recent dissolution. In 1918, Karl Liebknecht proclaimed a Socialist Republic from the balcony of a former royal palace on this spot. The balcony is incorporated in another large official building on the south side of Marx-Engels-Platz.

◆

WANNSEE
Map p 10–11
A great summertime destination for Berliners, the Wannsee offers sandy beaches, watersports and lakeside walks. There are two lakes, the Grosser and the

Wannsee, a watery playground

Kleiner Wannsee (the Great and the Little) which empty into the Havel River. On the shores, gracious residential suburbs have large villas surrounded by gardens, with sailing and rowing clubs dotted in between. Beside one of these boat clubs lies the grave of Heinrich von Kleist (1777–1811), the tormented writer of extraordinary plays and short stories. Born into an upper class Prussian military family, he had a strong death wish, and eventually entered a joyous, mutual suicide pact with a woman who was terminally ill. The grave is a few steps from Bismarckstrasse, close to the Wannsee S-Bahn.

◆

WEISSENSEE FRIEDHOF
Map p 30–1
The Weissensee Friedhof is a vast Jewish cemetery in East Berlin, not very far from the city centre, but with sloping woods, and birdsong ringing among the dense-packed gravestones. Behind the cemetery buildings, on the righthand side, a row of honour celebrates famous leaders of the Jewish community, among them the Berlin painter Lesser Ury (1861–1931). There is also a memorial to the resistance group led by Herbert Baum, all aged between 19 and 40, rounded up, tortured and executed in 1942–3. Here, more than anywhere, one senses the grievous loss to Berlin with the virtual extinction of its Jewish community. Men should wear hats or other head-covering.

Heads of dying warriors adorn the Zeughaus courtyard

♦♦♦
ZEUGHAUS
Unter den Linden 2, Map p 44–5
This palatial baroque building began its life as a store for weapons and arms. It was completed in 1706 and is one of the oldest buildings on Unter den Linden. The central courtyard is called the Schlüterhof, after the 22 heads of dying warriors sculpted by Andreas Schlüter. Concerts of classical music are held here in the summer on Thursday evenings. The **Museum für Deutsche Geschichte** (German History Museum) in the Zeughaus may be closed for alterations.
Open: Monday to Thursday

9:00A.M.–6:00P.M.; Saturday and Sunday 10:00A.M.–5:00P.M.

♦
ZOOLOGISCHER GARTEN
entry via Budapester Strasse or from Zoo Station (Hardenbergplatz)
Visitors with an equivalent at home may be less impressed than locals by the western city's zoo. The nocturnal animal house and aquarium (separate entrance fee) are the greatest attractions. There is another zoo, the **Tierpark**, in East Berlin.
Open: 9:00A.M.–6:30P.M.

POTSDAM AND SANSSOUCI

One of the best reasons for visiting Berlin is to go a little further and take in Potsdam too. This fascinating town and palace complex, on the extreme southwest periphery of Berlin, is packed with memories of Frederick the Great, whose elegant Schloss Sanssouci (Sanssouci Palace) is the main reason for a visit. In this century Potsdam has seen the rise of the great Babelsberg studios where many famous German films were made; the town also gave its name to the 1945 Potsdam Conference, at which the victorious Allies decided the shape of Europe. It lies just behind the southernmost point of the Wannsee among its own little group of Brandenburg lakes and hills.

Park Sanssouci

Frederick the Great's Sanssouci Schloss stands in Park Sanssouci, a 717-acre tract of hill and valley on the western edge of Potsdam. The whole of this is studded with palaces, villas,

Cecilienhof, a Prussian mock-Tudor mansion, was an imperial retreat

'romantic' ruins, orangeries and gardens of various kinds, and is delightful to wander in. Besides the places described in the entries below, there are others worth a look if you have time. Best, and earliest, is the Chinese teahouse (1754–7), topped by a mandarin under a parasol. Closer to the park entrance is the Friedenskirche or Peace Church (1845), psychologically important to Berliners but now in sad condition. Schloss Charlottenhof (1826) is a small palace in villa style, and the Römische Bäder (Roman Baths) of 1826–9 is another villa in Italianate style. There is an enormous orangery (1851–60) near the Neue Kammern, and other buildings in this area include an ancient mill and the pretty, four-level Drachenhaus (dragon-house) of 1770, based on the pagoda at Kew Gardens in London.

WHAT TO SEE

◆◆
CECILIENHOF
north of Potsdam
This fine half-timbered building set by a lakeside was the venue for the Potsdam Conference of 1945 and is much visited for that reason. Part of it is a hotel. Though rather too far to walk, the Cecilienhof is clearly signposted from Potsdam town. It was completed for the ruling Hohenzollern family in 1916 in imitation of an English Tudor mansion, and is shown to the public as it was at the time of the Conference. Stress is laid on the enormous loss of life during World War II. Visitors see the high hall where the delegations met – and the comfortable sitting room–libraries used by each team for preparation and study.
Open: daily 9:00A.M.–5:00P.M.
Closed: second and fourth Monday of each month.

◆◆
NEUES PALAIS
Park Sanssouci
After the exquisite quality of Sanssouci Palace, the New Palace of 1763–9 may well seem crude. It too was built by Frederick the Great however, both to house his guests and to assert, at terrifying cost, that his exhausted nation was not in fact exhausted by the Seven Years War.
Visitors pass from the grey vestibule into a shell-clad chamber, like an enormous, indoor grotto. After this comes what seems an infinity of ornate rooms, with court paintings and portraits. The tour concludes in the vast Marble Hall above the grotto, so heavy that the floor sagged when it was constructed, necessitating the speedy installation of supporting shell-clad arches below.
There is a pretty palace theatre (not shown on the tour) where concerts and plays are performed. Do not miss the palace café, around from the ticket office. You ring a bell for admittance and take your cream cake amid rococo splendours.
Open: as Schloss Sanssouci.

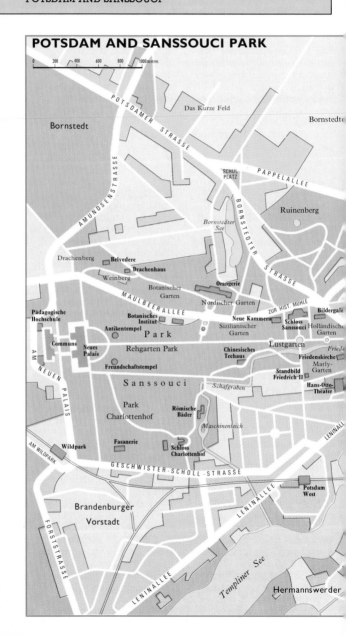

POTSDAM AND SANSSOUCI PARK

0   200   400   600   800   1000 metres

Potsdam

Bornstedt

Das Kurze Feld

Bornstedt

POTSDAMER STRASSE

SCHUL PLATZ

PAPPELALLEE

AMUNDSENSTRASSE

BORNSTEDTER STRASSE

Ruinenberg

Bornstedter See

Drachenberg

Belvedere

Drachenhaus

Weinberg

Botanischer Garten

Orangerie

MAULBEERALLEE

Nordischer Garten

ZUR HIST. MÜHLE

Pädagogische Hochschule

Botanisches Institut

Antikentempel

Neue Kammern

Bildergale

Sizilianischer Garten

Schloss Sanssouci

Holländische Garten

Park

Communs

Neues Palais

Rehgarten Park

Chinesisches Teehaus

Lustgarten

Friede

Friedenskirche

Marly-Garten

AM NEUEN PALAIS

Freundschaftstempel

Standbild Friedrich II

Sanssouci

Schafgraben

Hans-Otto-Theater

Park Charlottenhof

Römische Bäder

Muschinenteich

LENINALL

AM WILDPARK

Wildpark

Fasanerie

Schloss Charlottenhof

GESCHWISTER-SCHOLL-STRASSE

LENINALLEE

Potsdam West

Brandenburger Vorstadt

LENINALLEE

FORSTSTRASSE

Templiner See

LENINALLEE

Hermannswerder

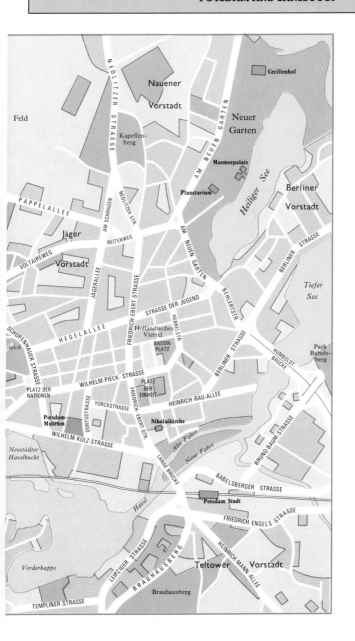

◆◆
POTSDAM

A British air raid, unleashed 200 years to the day after the foundation of Sanssouci, destroyed the centre of Potsdam, but several important buildings still survive – among them the restored Nikolaikirche (St Nicholas Church) by Schinkel. The court stables now house a film museum. In addition, there is a considerable quantity of 18th-century housing, thoroughly pleasing where restored. The red-brick and gabled Dutch Quarter was built between 1732 and 1752 to house Dutch textile workers. Closer to the Cecilienhof, there is an area of ample log houses in Russian style, built for the retinue of the various tsars who married into the Prussian ruling family. ·

◆◆◆
SCHLOSS SANSSOUCI
Park Sanssouci

What Frederick first intended was a summer palace where he could indulge in a life of letters and the arts *sans souci* – without care – while continuing the incessant administrative work that got him out of bed each day at 4:00A.M. He was already distanced from his wife, who never saw Sanssouci. He made the initial sketch himself and this was fleshed out by the architect Georg Wenzeslaus Knobelsdorff (1699–1753). Their collaboration resulted in one of the greatest triumphs of German rococo. Sadly, it ended two years later in a dispute which terminated Knobelsdorff's career. .
The success of Sanssouci

The exquisite Schloss Sanssouci

derives from its human scale allied to the greatest delicacy of decoration. The building is one storey only, and is best seen from the front. It stands at the top of a hillside, terraced for vines, leading down to a fountain and statuary. This view was planned by Frederick. The back of the building, where visitors enter, is ringed by a semi-circular colonnade, with a view of dramatically composed mock-ruins on the hill opposite. Visitors are taken around in groups, on a tour (in German only) which lasts about 40 minutes. First everyone puts on large felt slippers, then shuffles into the entrance hall to admire a graceful ceiling painting by the Swede

J Harper. A gallery to the left contains elegant paintings by pupils of Watteau. Note the bust of Frederick taken from his deathmask, revealing a face which is narrow, bony, quizzical and alert. His circular library is wood panelled under a sunburst ceiling, with fine bookcases in gilt and cedar. In the large adjoining chamber, divided by a pair of columns, look for the portrait of Frederick in a blue tunic, painted by Knobelsdorff. Next comes Frederick's music room, the ornate chamber where concerts were held each evening, with Frederick himself playing the flute, as often as not his own compositions. (He composed in the mornings, on a spinet, while having his hair attended to.) The whole wall surface of the music room is covered in an extraordinary filigree of rococo gilt. Johann Sebastian Bach was a visitor to Sanssouci and would have known this room; his son, C P E Bach, was for a period in residence and played concerts with the king. Among other rooms visited on the tour are the formal dining room beneath the dome, with plentiful marble and emblems of the arts, and a series of guest rooms, one decorated with wood carvings of parrots, a monkey and trails of flowers. One or other of these rooms (accounts vary) was occupied for long periods by Voltaire, the French philosopher, originally hero-worshipped by Frederick, but later teased to the point of maltreatment. The **Bildergalerie** (picture gallery) is on the right as you face the palace from the terraces. It was built by Büring, who also designed the Chinese teahouse, and contains mainly Renaissance and baroque paintings (*open*: summer only, 9:00A.M.–5:00P.M.). The **Dutch Gardens** lie below the terrace here. On the left of the palace, the **Neue Kammern** (New Chambers) were built as an orangery in 1747, and later converted into highly decorated guestrooms (*open*:

as Schloss Sanssouci, but closed Fridays). Beneath, on the righthand side as you face down the hill, is the **Sicilian Garden**.

Open: April to September 9:00A.M.–5:00P.M.; October, February and March 9:00A.M.–4:00P.M.; November to January 9:00A.M.–3:00P.M.

Closed: 12:30–1:00P.M. and first and third Monday in each month.

Chinese teahouse at Sanssouci

PEACE AND QUIET

Wildlife and Countryside in and around Berlin
by Paul Sterry

Although it is an unlikely seeming destination for anyone seeking relaxation or with an interest in natural history, in fact Berlin has much to offer within the city limits, and wildlife abounds further afield. Within Berlin itself there are numerous parks and gardens where you can relax and enjoy casual birdwatching, while the Grunewald Forest is a more extensive area of woodland within easy reach.

By travelling further, superb areas of boggy heathland and forest can be found. Many of these have escaped the worst ravages of the modern world, unlike similar habitats elsewhere in western Europe.

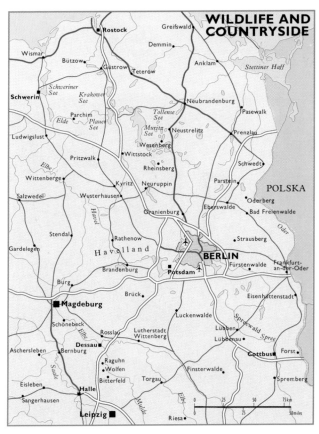

PEACE AND QUIET

The Tiergarten

The Tiergarten is an area of parkland containing the Zoo (Zoologischer Garten), which is open daily from 9:00A.M. until sunset. In addition to lakes, it has extensive woodland which, although natural in appearance, is almost entirely replanted, the original vegetation having been devastated in 1945 during the Battle of Berlin. The Tiergarten is a good place for leisurely strolls and a surprising number of birds can be seen within its boundaries. The nearest station is the Zoo Station; the whole area is bisected by Strasse des 17 Juni.

Grunewald Forest

The most convenient way to explore the forest is to take a bus to the station at Strandbad Wannsee. From here, visitors can explore the extensive woodland – the whole area covers 12.5 square miles (32 sq km) – and walk along the shores of the Havel Lakes. Much of the forest was cut down after the war for firewood but thanks to extensive replanting you would hardly know. Birds, mammals and insects can be found among the pines, oaks and birches and it is easy to find a secluded spot to sit and

A dappled path in the Grunewald

contemplate. The largest lake – Grunewaldsee – is beloved of swimmers but also attracts waterbirds such as grebes and ducks out of season. There are several smaller lakes within the boundaries of the forest.

Volkspark Friedrichschain

Near the junction of Friedenstrasse and Am Friedrichschain in what was formerly East Berlin, Volkspark Friedrichschain is an extensive park which is good for relaxing strolls. The wildlife interest is mainly limited to the human kind.

Weissensee

This lake and associated parkland area are northeast of Prenzlauer Berg, a suburb northeast of the centre of Berlin. It is a good place for strolling, with the chance of seeing wildfowl on the water.

Parks, Gardens and Lakes

In terms of wildlife, many of the smaller and more manicured parks and gardens will harbour little more than house sparrows, pigeons and starlings. However, some of the more extensive and overgrown areas attract a wider variety and have more to offer visitors with an interest in natural history.

In urban areas, woodland birds often become accustomed to the presence of man. Look for nuthatches and treecreepers feeding on trunks and branches. Both species have powerful feet that enable them to cling to vertical surfaces. Nuthatches are recognised by their squat appearance and

---

Thrush Nightingale

In the spring, large numbers of migrant birds arrive in the woodlands around Berlin to nest. Many of them, especially the warblers, have beautiful and distinctive songs with which they advertise their territories. However, perhaps the most attractive song – and certainly the loudest – belongs to a rather uniform brown bird known as a thrush nightingale or sprosser. Closely related to the nightingale of southern and western Europe, the smallish thrush nightingale has an even louder song than its relative. It comprises a mixture of loud 'chok' notes and a series of high-pitched and drawn-out calls repeated over and over again.

---

blue-grey and tan plumage. Treecreepers, on the other hand, have streaked brown plumage and a thin, down-curved bill.

Among the smaller birds, look for robins, great tits, coal tits, chaffinches and woodpeckers. During migration times (April and May, then September and October) a wide range of other species, including warblers and flycatchers, pass through on their way to and from their breeding territories in northern Europe and their wintering grounds in southern Europe and Africa.

On lakes and ponds in Berlin, look for birds such as mallards, tufted ducks, pochards, coots and black-headed gulls. In the autumn and winter, several other species of wildfowl may appear, including goldeneyes, teal and shoveler.

PEACE AND QUIET

Although mammals have largely disappeared from the centre of Berlin, red squirrels can sometimes be seen in more remote areas of woodland around the outskirts of the city. They have orange-red fur, a tufted tail and tufted tips to the ears.

Further Afield
Compared to many parts of Europe, much of what formerly comprised East Germany is comparatively unspoilt. It is a land of heathland and boggy marsh, of forest and lake.

White-tailed eagle

Here, some of Europe's more threatened plants and animals survive and many are more abundant than anywhere else in Europe. Although almost any lake or area of forest or marsh that looks unspoilt is likely to harbour interesting wildlife, the following are some of the more important sites within reach of Berlin.

Schweriner See and Krakower See
These two lakes lie east of Schwerin, reached by driving northwest from Berlin on the E15 to Ludwigslust and then heading north to Schwerin. The waters of the lakes are nutrient rich and extremely productive, and harbour large numbers of fish and frogs. Reed-beds and alder carr woodlands line the shore, and gulls and terns breed on some of the protected islands. Ducks and geese pass through on migration and some stay the winter. Ospreys feed on the fish in the lakes, while white-

White-tailed Eagle
With a wingspan of about eight feet (250cm), the white-tailed eagle is the largest bird of prey to be seen in Germany. Adults are unmistakable in flight: with their broad wings they resemble a huge door in flight, and the white, wedge-shaped tail is characteristic. Juveniles, however, have brown tails and their shape must be used to identify them. White-tailed eagles breed around lakes and marshes and build large stick nests in trees. They feed on birds such as ducks as well as fish and carrion.

tailed eagles thrive on both the fish and the birds of the region.

Neubrandenburg and Neustrelitz

These two towns are north of Berlin and can be reached by driving on the E96 from the city. To the west of the road between the two towns are a series of lakes surrounded in places by marsh and woodland; explore this area using minor roads. The landscape shows much evidence of glaciation: the country is smooth and rolling, the lakes are shallow and the glacial moraines have woods of birch, alder, pine and oak. Sites which are particularly noteworthy include Galenbecker See, Tollense See and Kleines Haff, near Neubrandenburg, and Serrahn, to the east of Neustrelitz. On your way back to Berlin it is worth detouring to Wesenberg, southwest of Neustrelitz, and taking the minor road south to Rheinsberg. Interesting bog plants can be seen in all these areas, and grey herons, white-tailed eagles, lesser spotted eagles and cranes breed.

Brandenburg

Brandenburg lies on the flat Havel Plain west of Berlin. It is a region of lakes and marshes and the haunt of wetland birds and flowers. Several lakes can be found around the perimeter of Brandenburg itself. One of the most interesting is the Reitzer See, to the southeast. The lake itself is the haunt of wildfowl while the surrounding marsh has an interesting flora.

Common crane spying out the land

Urwald Breitefenn

This area of virgin forest lies northeast of Berlin between Oderberg and Parstein. To reach it, head out of the city on the road to Bad Freienwalde. Pass through the town and before you reach Altglietzen turn left to Oderberg and on to Parstein. In addition to forest, there is marsh and open water here. At Plagefenn, northeast of Eberswalde, is a reserve where wet woodland and open water (Plagesee) can be found.

Schlaubetal

To reach this valley drive east from Berlin on the E8 to Frankfurt-an-der-Oder and then south to Eisenhüttenstadt. Here, visitors will find heathland, lakes and forest and a wealth of bird and plant life.

PEACE AND QUIET

Lübben

Near Lübben can be found the Lower Spree Forest (Spreewald), on the edge of which is a nature reserve at Kriegbusch. The River Spree ensures a rich growth of marsh plants in the alder carr woodland, with oaks and hornbeams growing on drier ground. Storks nest in the trees here.

Untere Mulde

The River Mulde between Dessau and Bitterfeld is a good area to look for beavers. Drive south from Berlin on the E6 and, in the vicinity of Dessau take the minor road to Raguhn which runs parallel to the river on its east side. Part of the area is a nature reserve set up to protect the forest and beavers.

Bogs and Heathland

Heathland is a type of habitat that is found on sandy soils which are acidic in nature, low in nutrients and often well drained. To the south and east of Berlin, tracts of heathland still persist and species of heathers are typical plants of this terrain. Where valley bottoms are found, water collects and bogs form; these habitats are rich in interesting plant life. Sundews – plants with sticky leaves – supplement their diet by catching and digesting insects, and there are often large tracts of cottongrass, bog myrtle and *Sphagnum* moss studded with heath spotted orchids in summer. Waders and ducks breed in the bogs and, where patches of woodland form, birds such as bluethroats and hen harriers can be found.

A long-leaved sundew taking lunch

Forest birds

Forests and woodlands around Berlin harbour a wide variety of interesting birds including some which are quite difficult to see in western Europe. Golden orioles are widespread and often common summer visitors. Although the males are bright yellow in colour – females are rather duller – they are difficult to see among dappled foliage. However, their loud, fluty song carries a considerable distance and is quite unmistakable. Many birds of prey also breed in the region. Red kites and black kites – both recognised by their forked tails – are often common, and lesser spotted eagles are sometimes seen. Although juveniles have white spots, adults, despite their name, are a rather uniform brown colour. In flight, they have broad wings and a short, wedge-shaped tail.

FOOD AND DRINK

Traditional German cuisine is not in the top ranks of European gastronomy, but what it lacks in subtlety, it makes up in quantity. The *Berliner Schlachteplatte* consists of boiled pork, liver sausage and pigs' kidneys with potatoes and *sauerkraut* (pickled cabbage). *The* Berlin meat dish is *Eisbein*, knuckle of pork with *sauerkraut* and *Erbspüree* (mashed peas). Near forest areas, you might find *Wildschweinbraten* – roast wild boar; *Schlesisches Himmerlreich* means either roast pork or goose with potato dumplings in gravy; *Spanferkel* is suckling pig; and *Königsbergerklopse* means meatballs in cream. Potatoes are served up as *Kartoffelpuffer* (fried potato cakes), *Kartoffelsuppe* (potato soup with chunks of bacon and a parsley garnish) and *Pellkartoffeln mit Quark* (jacket potatoes with curd cheese, plus optional linseed oil). Fish figures large in local cuisine, with pickled herring, the more delicate *Matjeshering* (raw herring fillets with apple, onion and gherkins in cream) and *Aal grün* – eels in herb sauce, possibly caught in the nearby Havel.
There are numerous types of traditional bread.
All this has been displaced in many restaurants by the 'new German cuisine', which emphasises fresh products, imaginative recipes and smaller portions; and the range of other national cuisines is large. There are any number of Italian restaurants, and Turkish food is popular as well, both as served in *schnell imbiss* (fast food) bars on every street corner, and in reasonably priced restaurants. There is also a choice of Chinese, Thai, Egyptian, Spanish, French, Japanese and American.

Where to Eat

In a city that stays up all night, there is always somewhere to get a decent meal. Possibilities range from the *Kneipe* (corner pub and snack bar), to cafés

Coffee at Kranzler on the Ku'damm

FOOD AND DRINK

(some open all day and most of the night for drinks and meals), as well as rather more formal restaurants. In between meals, there is always the *Konditorei* (cake and coffee shop). Most famous of these is the **Kranzler**, one of the cafés where intellectuals met from the early years of the 19th century. Formerly in the Friedrichstrasse in the East, it was transferred after World War II to the Ku'damm in the West.

Every *Rathaus*, or town hall, has a café in the basement, called the *Ratskeller*. This is usually a large civic establishment serving good food at a reasonable price.

Mealtimes

Breakfast in Berlin is a day-long event, served in some cafés from 8:30A.M. until midnight. German breakfast is normally a selection of cold meats, pâté and cheese with a variety of bread. Most Berliners have both lunch (the main meal of the day) and their evening meal relatively early – at noon and 6:00P.M. respectively.

Drink

Berlin is predominantly a beer city with a couple of well-known local breweries – Berliner Kindl and Schultheiss (the latter now part of a larger national brewery). Locally brewed East German beers, once esteemed by experts, are now in shorter supply given the craze for all things Western. If you want draught beer, ask for 'Bier vom Fass'. A popular summer drink is the

Berliner Weisse mit Schuss, a low-alcohol beer flavoured with a shot of pink raspberry juice or extract of green woodruff. Germany also produces a wide range of Rhine-type white wines, some of them fruity. Red wines, all from the southwest, are very few.

Restaurant Districts

In the West, the district around the Europa-Center and the Ku'damm is full of bars and restaurants patronised by tourists. The area north of Savignyplatz is equally rich in bars, cafés and restaurants. Here the clientele are students and young locals. Nollendorf is popular with the young; Kreuzberg is the heart of 'alternative' Berlin.

In the East, there is no shortage of places within the Mitte district. The Nikolaiviertel area especially has many bars and restaurants worth sampling. Prenzlauer Berg district has growing nightlife, bars and restaurants.

West

Around Ku'damm

Cafe Möhring, Kurfürstendamm 213 (tel: 881 20 75). Like the Café Kranzler, this cake and coffee shop is a traditional institution. Elegant Jugendstil style and tinkling piano; but slow and sloppy service.

Fofi Estiatorio, Fasanenstrasse 70 (tel:881 87 85). An excellent Greek restaurant patronised by artists whose work is displayed in local galleries (or who would like to be). Welcoming service.

Hardtke, Meinekestrasse 27 (tel: 881 98 27). This old-fashioned Berlin-style restaurant – dark wood panelling, old oil lamps hanging over wooden tables, and waiters in waistcoats and aprons – serves traditional food at reasonable prices. Also at Hubertusallee 48, Wilmersdorf.

Joe am Ku'damm,
Kurfürstendamm 225 (tel: 883 62 73). A lot of blue neon lighting seems to pull in a young crowd. Not somewhere to return to every night, but much used by new arrivals.

Kempinski-Eck,
Kurfürstendamm 27 (tel: 884 340). Sane, sober and elegant. A good place to watch the world go by; not cheap but worth it.

Wintergarten, Fasanenstrasse 23 (tel: 882 54 14). The house is a meeting place for anybody involved in books, with a bookshop in the basement and a café extension – open to all. Excellent food, good value.

Around Savignyplatz
Café Hardenberg,
Hardenbergstrasse (tel: 312 33 30). A young person's café, full of undergraduates in serious discussion and even more serious beer drinking. Bicycle park outside; loud music.

Court Carrée, Savignyplatz 5 (tel: 312 52 38). On a broad corner of the Savignyplatz, with views of the lively square. Good French food, garden seating in summer.

Dicke Wirtin, Carmerstrasse 9 (tel: 312 49 52). Popular dark brown Berlin pub, with walls covered in posters and paintings and mirrors. Serves cheap and filling soups.

Dralles, Schluterstrasse 59. Pleasant bar in 1950s décor.

Kant Billard Café, on corner of Kantstrasse and Leibnitstrasse, for avid billiard players.

Cafe Möhring is a place to sit and drink in the atmosphere

FOOD AND DRINK

Paris Bar, Kantstrasse 152 (tel: 313 80 52). A pleasant establishment, rather living off its earlier reputation as the gathering place of the chic and upwardly mobile.

Rococo, Knesebeckstrasse 92. A popular Italian restaurant with a convivial atmosphere. Moderate prices and live guitar music.

Schwarzes Café, Kantstrasse 148 (tel: 313 80 38). A 24-hour bar which only closes during

There are plenty of informal eating places in the centre

the day on Tuesday. Plenty of atmosphere and good food.

Shell, Knesebeckstrasse 22 (tel: 312 83 10). White tablecloths, bentwood chairs, and plain wooden floors – the decor is simple, but this restaurant is lively, cheerful and always busy.

Wirtshaus Wuppke, Schluterstrasse 21

(tel: 313 81 62). Old-fashioned German pub.

Around Nollendorf

Carib, Motzstrasse 30. If you can fight your way through the palms, try the Caribbean specialities of curried goat, *akee* and salt fish. A choice of exotic cocktails to start with.

Einstein, Kurfürstenstrasse 58 (tel: 261 50 96). A large old-fashioned café on the ground floor of a neo-classical house which once belonged to Henny Porten, star of silent films. Young waiters in tails serve an artistic and literary set. Gardens to the rear.

Strada, Potsdamerstrasse 131. One large, simply furnished room. Excellent food and friendly service.

Around Kreuzberg

Café am Ufer, Paul-Lincke-Ufer 42–3. Popular café on the ground floor of a splendidly renovated house beside the canal.

Die Rote Harfe, Oranienstrasse 13. Cheap German beer, Guinness or steaming cups of cappucino and cheerful company. Despite a hot political reputation, it is the sort of place you can bring a baby in a stroller. Food upstairs. Similar establishment at the **Elefanta** next door.

Genclik Kollari, Oranienstrasse. Good Turkish food. The rest of the customers are usually Turkish, mostly men, gathering to chat over cups of tea. Welcoming atmosphere, no alcohol.

Gino's La Bohéme, Nostitzstrasse 49. A little neighbourhood music bar which also serves good food from 6:00P.M. to 2:00A.M.

Max und Moritz, Oranienstrasse 162. Sober and traditional. Unusually for Berlin, it asks anybody not actually eating to sit at the bar rather than an empty table. Blackboard menu.

Mora Café, Grossbeerenstrasse 57. A gallery café of three adjoining rooms, hung with pictures which can be bought from the Manfred Gresler gallery next door.

East

Mitte/Nikolaiviertel

Berliner Ratskeller, Rotes Rathaus, Rathausstrasse. The civic café/restaurant of the Red Town Hall is divided into a beer restaurant at one end and a wine restaurant (more expensive) at the other. Dancing on Wednesdays, Thursdays and Sundays after 7:00P.M.

Café Bauer, Grand Hotel, Friedrichstrasse (tel:209 232 53). Old fashioned and elegant, with a rather staid atmosphere and excellent service.

Fernsehturm (TV Tower) Restaurant, Alexanderplatz. The 679-foot (207m) tower has a revolving café/restaurant above the viewing gallery. Great views, food and drink for those with calm stomachs.

Operncafé, Unter den Linden 5 (tel: 200 0256). Coffee and cakes to one side, upscale bar to the other and restaurant upstairs. This most elegant of Berlin's cafés has terrace seating in the summer.

FOOD AND DRINK/SHOPPING

Restaurant Ephraim Palais,
Poststrasse 16 (tel: 217 13164).
In a splendid location adjoining
the palace and backing on to
the Spree canal. Discreet
plush and comfort inside.
Turmstuben, Französicher
Dom, Platz der Akademie. As
you climb the tower of the
Französicher Dom, you will
come upon this charming, cosy
café-restaurant.
Zum Nussbaum,
Propstrasse/Am Nussbaum
(tel: 2171 3328). An old Berlin
pub, modelled on one
frequented by the local, much-
loved cartoonist, Heinrich Zille
(1858–1929). The whole of this
steeply gabled house in front
of Nikolaikirche has been
entirely restored.
Zum Paddenwirt,
Nikolaikircheplatz 6
(tel: 2171 3231). Just behind the
Nikolaikirche, a comfortable
old-style bar and eatery with
good German home cooking.
Also restored.

Around Prenzlauerberg
Aphrodite, Schönhauser Allee
61 (tel: 448 1707). Modern,
elegant restaurant serving
New German cooking.
Kaffee Stube,
Husemannstrasse 6. Small
neighbourhood café which
serves light meals in the newly
renovated Husemannstrasse.
Lolott, Schönhauser Allee 56.
An example of the chic new
eating places springing up
everywhere on this street.
Restauration 1900, corner of
Husemannstrasse and
Wörtherstrasse. A classy
restaurant, supposedly
patronised by artists.

SHOPPING

At present the visitor will find
the best shopping in the old
West of the city. What
consumerism exists in the East
can be seen making a slow
and painful appearance, for
example along the
Schönhauser Allee, on the
western edge of the
Prenzlauer Berg district. Here,
where there was precious little
on sale before 1989, there are
now greengrocers with
oranges and bananas,
pharmacies with Western
hygiene products and even a
Japanese car showroom.
Meissen porcelain is produced
in the East and sold, among
other places, in a speciality
Meissen shop close to where
Friedrichstrasse crosses Unter
den Linden. There is no price
advantage, though, in buying
here rather than in West
Berlin. The biggest shop in
East Berlin remains the
Centrum department store on
the Alexanderplatz. Once a
showpiece for the relative
cheapness of Eastern bloc
shopping, it is now an ordinary
department store. Generally
cheap and cheerful, it offers
goods from everywhere and
even boasts a travel agency.

Basics
There are excellent shopping
areas, patronised by locals, in
the main streets of all the
various boroughs and districts,
for example: Karl-Marx-Strasse
in Neukölln with cheap
boutiques where you might
find leather goods, particularly
at the Hermannplatz U-Bahn
end; Wilmersdorfer Strasse in

Charlottenburg, for a range of shops and department stores; Schlossstrasse, near the U-Bahn in Steglitz; and the pedestrianised Old Town in Spandau. In addition, there is the Europa-Center, a glitzy rather than glamorous building of shops and offices just by the Breitscheidplatz, with a variety of middle-range goods for sale.

Upscale

The most expensive shops are to be found in the Ku'damm, near the Breitscheidplatz end, and in the smaller streets running off this thoroughfare. No visitor should come to Berlin without entering the portals of its most famous shop – the Ka De We, short for Kaufhaus des Westens, a department store established since the 1880s in Wittenbergplatz. The sixth floor is entirely given over to food and drink, both to take home and for immediate consumption (pick your own fresh fish, to be grilled while

The Europa-Center

you wait, enjoying a glass of *sekt*, Germany's champagne equivalent). Locals vote the sales staff the most helpful and knowledgeable of any. The Wertheim department store, run by the same company as Ka De We, offers a smaller range of goods at lower prices, at Kurfürstendamm 231. Peek and Cloppenberg, next door to Ka De We, is excellent for clothes.

Immediately you turn off the Ku'damm into Fasanenstrasse, the atmosphere is altogether more refined. Valentino Garavani at no 74 sells small and expensive gifts. This is the place to buy that special souvenir of Berlin – a solid gold bear. Past the pink brick façade of the Literaturhaus and the Käthe Kollwitz Museum, you can peep into some of the most prestigious art galleries in Berlin. There is designer fashion at Patrick Hellmann (no 26), and designer jewellery at Cartier's. A small passage leading into Uhlandstrasse has another gallery and more upscale shops. Stop for a coffee at the Wiener Kaffeehaus before going on to look at the Oriental fabrics at Himmel Auf Erden (Heaven on Earth). Boutique Simone at the end of the passage sells women's fashions for special occasions.

In Uhlandstrasse itself, the Perlen Bar stocks everything for the do-it-yourself jeweller. Stop at no 38, Musikalienhandlung, for sheet music and records.

On Ludwigkirchstrasse, Falbala sells secondhand

clothes from the 1920s and 1930s, and Das Spiel has any game that can be made of wood. On Pariser Strasse, Galerie Janssen is a homo-erotic gallery and bookshop, Champ sells excellent men's clothes in German style, and you can buy anything sporty from Citysport. Continue along Pariser Strasse, and into Bleibtreustrasse, for more exclusive fashion and accessory shops, a few seconds away from the Ku'damm.

Budget Secondhand Clothes

The Garage, a huge basement warehouse in Ahornstrasse, Nollendorf, sells racks of shirts, jeans, coats, hats and shoes by the kilo. If you cannot find precisely what you are looking for, there is also Kauf's im Kilo, Hermanstrasse 1–3, and Second Coming, Motzstrasse 15, among others. Most secondhand clothes shops open every day at about 11:00A.M. and are patronised by young people and students. For better quality and secondhand designer clothes, try Macy's and Secondo, both in Mommsenstrasse, and Falbala (see **Upscale**, above).

Markets

The Nollendorf Flohmarkt (fleamarket) operates from ex-railway carriages in the old Nollendorfplatz S-Bahn station. This is a good place to pick up antique bits and pieces as well as secondhand books, records and clothes (closed on Tuesday). A tram runs from here to the old S-Bahn station

at Bülowstrasse, where there is a Turkish Bazaar. This is a much smaller affair catering mostly to Turkish Berliners, selling Turkish pop music, jewellery and wedding clothes.

The weekend market at Strasse des 17 Juni, near the Tiergarten S-Bahn, sells mostly poor quality goods, but its central position ensures an interesting crowd. Kreuzberg has the Sunday Krempelmarkt at Reichpietschufer, and Wilmersdorf holds a Sunday secondhand market at Fehrbelliner Platz.

There is an open air food market in every district, often in the square outside the *rathaus* (town hall).

For colour and spectacle, go to the Turkish market held at Maybachufer in Neukölln, on

Nollendorf Flohmarkt occupies old railway carriages

Tuesday and Friday noon–6:00P.M. Here you will find olives, cheeses, live chickens and rabbits, and always the scent of spices.

Specialities

Speciality shops tend to be grouped in certain areas. For German antique furniture try the shops in Keithstrasse and Eisenacher Strasse in Schöneberg. For books, the area near the Techische Universität, around Knesebeckstrasse and Hardenbergstrasse, has shops which stock German and foreign language books in specialist subjects. For new fashion, jewellery and furniture design, keep an eye on the art and craft shops in the

Schöneberg/Kreuzberg area.
The Berliner Zinnfiguren
(Berlin Tin Soldier),
Knesebeckstrasse 88, is an old-
established shop with over
30,000 model soldiers for sale,
ready moulded or for home
moulding. Fine porcelain is
sold in all the better shops.
The showrooms of the
Königliche Porzellanmanufaktur
(Royal Porcelain Factory) are
on Wegelystrasse by the
Tiergarten S-Bahn; East Berlin
has a Meissen porcelain shop
(see above).
For souvenirs of Berlin, the
shops attached to museums
always have some small and
interesting items. The plaster-
casting shop of the State
Museum at Sophie-Charlotten-
Strasse 17–18 sells copies of
notable busts and statues at a
reasonable price.

The Palasthotel is on the Spree

ACCOMMODATION

There is a wide choice of
accommodation in Berlin,
ranging from expensive,
luxury hotels to cheap
pensions and *Privat Unterkunft*
(bed and breakfast). In West
Berlin there is a nucleus
around Zoo Station and the
Ku'damm, but the excellent
public transport network
makes a hotel outside the
centre possible. East Berlin
has always had quality hotels,
and more pension
accommodation is becoming
available all the time.
However, the visitor who
chooses an inexpensive stay in
the East, particularly outside
the centre, should not yet
expect the standards
considered normal in the
West.
It is now possible to book a
hotel in any part of Berlin
directly, or, if you prefer, via

the tourist office in Berlin, at least two weeks before your trip, at Verkehrsamt Berlin, Europa-Center, 1000 Berlin 30 (tel: 262 6031). Explain how long you want to stay and the type and price of accommodation you are after. A small fee is charged. For longer stays, the Mitwohnzentrale apartment sharing centre can arrange accommodation in a variety of private properties: the address is 3rd floor, Ku'damm Eck, Kurfürstendamm 227–8, Berlin (tel: (030) 882 6694).

Expensive
West
Bristol Hotel Kempinski, Kurfürstendamm 27, Berlin 15 (tel: 884 34-0). This modern hotel evokes an earlier splendour. Classy and luxurious, favoured by knowledgeable transatlantic visitors.

Inter-Continental Berlin, Budapesterstrasse 2, Berlin 30 (tel: 26020). Berlin's biggest hotel, with 600 rooms. Near the Europa-Center and Tiergarten, with all the usual facilities of a very expensive hotel.

Steigenberger Berlin, Los Angeles Platz 1, Berlin 30 (tel: 21 080). Large and efficient, central but quietly situated.

East
Domhotel, Mohrenstrasse 30 (tel: 20 98 0/22 040). New, luxury, central hotel with eight restaurants. Light and spacious with greenery and running water. There are special rooms for non-smokers and guests with disabilities.

Grand Hotel, Friedrichstrasse 158–64, 1080 Berlin (tel: 20920). Arguably the best hotel in all Berlin. Hotel restaurant on the first floor; separate luxury restaurant on the seventh; shopping arcade and fitness club.

Palasthotel, Karl-Liebknecht Strasse 5, 1020 Berlin (tel: 2410). Ideal position facing Museumsinsel and the cathedral, but wins no prizes for service.

Potsdam
Schloss Cecilienhof, Neuer Garten, Potsdam (tel: 23141-41). This comfortable hotel is part of the Cecilienhof which hosted the Potsdam Conference in 1945, and is surrounded by attractive grounds. Out of town – you would need your own transportation.

Medium
West
Art Hotel Sorat, Joachimstaler Strasse 28-9, Berlin 12 (tel: 88 44 70). Public areas and bedrooms are decorated with paintings and sculptures. This hotel (at the very top of the medium price range) is for design-conscious aesthetes. Another in this chain is to be built on the northern shores of the Tegeler See.

Kronprinz, Kronprinzendamm 1, Berlin 31 (tel: 89 60 30). At the western end of the Ku'damm. The emphasis is on up-to-date service in the ambience of 19th-century Berlin, and there is a delightful beer garden.

Charlot, Giesebrechtstrasse 17, Berlin 12 (tel: 323 40 51). An

ACCOMMODATION

excellent value hotel for its central position near the Adenauerplatz U-bahn stop.
Meineke, Meinekestrasse 10, Berlin 15 (tel: 882 8111). Old fashioned, not luxurious, not expensive, but comfortable and near the Ku'damm.

East
Adria, Friedrichstrasse 134, 1040 Berlin (tel: 280 5105). Central position, medium prices and decent restaurant. Elevator suitable for wheelchairs.
Newa, Invalidenstrasse 115, 1040 Berlin (tel: 282 5461). About 10 minutes' ride from the city centre. Not all rooms have a private bath or shower.

Cheap
Lower-priced hotels and pensions may not have a bath or shower in every room.

West
Artemisia Hotel, Brandenburgische Strasse 18, Berlin 31 (tel: 87 89 05 or 87 63 73). A central, women-only hotel on two upper floors. Pleasant and good value.
Bogota, Schlüterstrasse 45, Berlin 15 (tel: 881 50 01). A reasonably priced, central hotel. Comfortable rooms and friendly atmosphere.
Centrum Pension Berlin, Kantstrasse 31, Berlin 12 (tel: 31 6153). A family-run hotel which welcomes children. In Charlottenburg, a 10-minute walk from Zoo Station.
Econtel Berlin, Sömmeringstrasse 24, Berlin 10 (tel: 34 40 01). Near the Schloss Charlottenburg. Cots, bottle-warming facilities, and

discounts for children sharing their parents' room; easy public transport to centre.
Hotel-Pension Bernhard, Bernardstrasse 9, Berlin 31 (tel: 854 30 81). A small but excellent new hotel near the U-Bahn Bundesplatz.
Hotelpension Dittberner, Wielanstrasse 25, Berlin 15 (tel: 881 64 84). On the upper floor of a building that also houses an art gallery.
Hotel-Pension Wittelsbach, Wittelsbacherstrasse 22, Berlin 31 (tel: 87 63 45). Near U-Bahn Konstanze Strasse. A family hotel, with a playroom indoors and a garden play area.
Mark Hotel, Meinekestrasse 18-19, Berlin 12 (tel: 8 80 02-0). Central, clean and efficient. Cheerful in the midst of coming and going of young parties.
Pension München, Güntselstrasse 62, Berlin 31 (tel: 854 22 26). Small, upper-floor pension, three stops on U-Bahn from Zoo Station.
Pension Niebuhr, Niebuhrstrasse 74, Berlin 12 (tel: 324 9595). Situated in a quiet area but close to Ku'damm; welcomes children.

East
Christliches Hospiz, Augustrasse 82, 1040 Berlin (tel: 280 5145/282 5321). Low-priced accommodation, run by the Church, a 10-minute ride from central Berlin. *Bureau de change.*
Hospiz am Bahnhof, Friedrichstrasse, Albrechtstrasse 8, 1040 Berlin (tel: 282 5396). A popular, convenient location, so book well in advance. Restaurant.

CULTURE, ENTERTAINMENT AND NIGHTLIFE

As well as regular festivals, including the Berlin Film Festival, the city offers some of the best classical music, opera and theatre in the world. There also exists a ferment of activity in experimental theatre, experimental dance, jazz, rock, pop and international music, together with circus arts and puppetry. Since the Wall came down, Berlin's tradition of political satire seems to have acquired a sharper edge. All this runs alongside the light plays and comedies of the commercial theatre, the discos, casinos and nightclubs. Here, the Berlin predilection is for 'travestie' or drag shows – they are almost inescapable, their offerings ranging from the humorously naughty to the extremely lewd.

Berlin has two good listings magazines covering all the arts, high and low – *Zitty* and *Tip*. The Tourist Office publishes a monthly *Berlin Programme*.

For the most popular shows, it is almost impossible to get tickets at short notice from regular box offices. Use the ticket agencies or Theaterkassen, at the Europa-Center, Tauentzientstrasse 9 (tel: 261 70 51/52), Ka De We department store, Tauentzienstrasse 21 (tel: 882 7360), and Wertheim, Kurfürstendamm 231 (tel: 882 2500); or agency offices at Meinekestrasse 25 (tel: 882 7611), Kurfürstendamm 24 (tel: 882 7360), or Rankestrasse 1 (tel: 881 4507).

The Berlin Philharmonie's hall

CULTURE, ENTERTAINMENT AND NIGHTLIFE

Classic style: Deutsche Staatsoper

Classical Music
West

Classical music is dominated by the Berlin Philharmonie under conductor Claudio Abbado. Their proper home is the dramatic Philharmonie building in the Tiergarten – designed by Hans Scharoun and worth a look in its own right. The seats go right round the concert hall, in a plan inspired by the way people gather naturally around the source of music.

Tickets for major concerts are difficult to obtain, but there are always smaller concerts or recitals. The Deutsche Oper, Bismarckstrasse 34 offers a classical music programme as well as opera and ballet. The city is also full of small orchestras and music groups performing regularly.

East

The main concert hall is the Berliner Schauspielhaus, Platz der Akademie. The Berliner Sinfonie Orchester is leader of the pack among the music-makers of the East, closely followed by the orchestra of the Komische Oper, Behrenstrasse 55-7. Staatskapelle is the prestigious State Choir at Unter den Linden 7, and the Deutsche Staatsoper, next door on Unter den Linden, is the operatic equivalent. Tickets for concerts are available from the Reisebüro on Alexanderplatz.

Jazz, Rock and Folk
West

Deutschlandhalle, Eissporthalle and the ICC

Berlin are the largest of Berlin's many conference venues which are also used for music. The Congress Hall in the Tiergarten serves the same dual function.

The Waldbühne, the huge amphitheatre near the Olympic Stadium, attracts world famous artists. The 'Tempodrom' is two tents set up in the Tiergarten to house a variety of entertainment, including live music in the summer.

Jazz enthusiasts are well catered for at the Badenscher Hof café-restaurant, Badenscherstrasse 29 in Schöneberg district. Flöz, Nassauische Strasse 37, Quasimodo, Kantstrasse 12a and Blues Café, Körnerstrasse 11 are among the most popular places to hear jazz. Go-In, Bleibtreustrasse 17, has international folk music: you might hear Scottish laments or Chinese peasant songs. The Irish Inn, Damaschkestrasse 28, serves folk music and Guinness to a cosmopolitan audience. Moderately famous rock bands perform at the Metropol, Nollendorf Platz 5. The Loft, part of the Metropol, hosts smaller bands with a more experimental flavour.

East

Large concert venues like the Radrennbahn in Weissensee have often hosted bands and performers well known in the West. Many of the major clubs provide wide ranging arts programmes with music as one constituent. Here is a small selection: Club 29, Rosa-Luxemburg-Strasse 29; Haus der jungen Talente, Klosterstrasse 68–70; Erich-Franz-Club, Schönhauser Allee 36–9, and Kreiskulturhaus 'Prater', Kastanienallee 7–9, both in Prenzlauer Berg.

Nightclubs
West

Nightclubs in the West are abundant with a rapid turnover of name and style. Few charge an entrance fee. This is a small selection:

Abraxas, Kantstrasse 134, has free entry and the rhythm is mostly Latin. At Blue Note, Courbierestrasse 13, there is a small charge on Friday and Saturday night, with Latin and jazz a speciality. Dschungel, Nürnbergerstrasse 53, has been voted one of the best by those in the know, with Cha-Cha, next door at Nürnberger-strasse 50, second. Sox, Oranienstrasse 39, is for young people; Linientreu, Budapesterstrasse 40, and Metropol, Nollendorfplatz 5, are for an older crowd.

East

Nightlife is not very developed in the old East, although things are changing. You will probably find the most lively night spots in the Prenzlauer Berg and Pankow areas. Expect things to be more conservative than in the West. Try the Yucca Bar, in Pankow at Neumannstrasse 136; Café Lolott and Café Nord, both on Schönhauser Allee; Ballhaus Berlin, Chausseestrasse 108, in Mitte, with table telephones; and, in Mitte, Clärchens Ballhaus,

Auguststrasse 24–5, and Jo-Jo, Wilhelm-Pieck-Strasse 216.

Cabaret and Revue

The most extravagant variety revue show is in the East, in the Friedrichstadtpalast (tel: 283 6474). Here, world class performers share the programme with dancing girls and variety acts. The Kleine Revue – the Small Revue – in the same building, is more intimate and adult. After the show ends at midnight, the stage becomes a dance floor. The Europa-Center is the home of La Vie En Rose revue: a lot of dancing girls in feathers and pearls and not much else. Also in the Europa-Center is the political cabaret, Die Stachelschweine – the Hedgehogs – considered not nearly sharp enough by some. Die Wühlmäuse (the Voles) on Lietzenburgerstrasse, is considered much better value as political cabaret. In the East, Die Distel (the Thistle), in Friedrichstrasse 101, with its secondary stage in the Potsdamer Kabarett, Schopenhauerstrasse 27, is said to be unrivalled. Die Distel and Wühlmäuse may be combined. You need good knowledge of German and German politics to appreciate these shows, which have a long established history in Berlin.

Other cabarets include Kleinkunstbühne Intimes Theater, Oranienstrasse 162; and Theater im Keller, Weserstrasse 211. There is a *Spielbank* (casino) in the Europa-Center.

Dance

West Berlin's one ballet company is attached to the Deutsche Oper. There is, though, a strong tradition of experimental and modern dance in the city. It was in Berlin that Isadora Duncan opened her first school. The Tanzfabrik, Mockernstrasse 68, in Kreuzberg, was formed as a collective to practise and teach dance theatre and experimental dance forms, and has a considerable reputation. The Tanz Tangente company on Kuhligshofstrasse 4 also performs and teaches. The emphasis here is mainly on American and jazz techniques.

Theatre
West

Opera and ballet performances take place in the Deutsche Oper, Bismarckstrasse 35. Across the road, the Schiller Theatre, Bismarckstrasse 110 offers the best of theatre and experimental work in their studio. The repertoire includes ancient and modern classics from all countries. Another prestigious company is the Schaubühne am Lehniner Platz, Kurfürstendamm 153, formed by a core of East German actors and directors who left the East long before the Wall came down. For musicals and comedies try the Komödie and the Theater am Kurfürstendamm, both at Kurfürstendamm 206. The Theater des Westens, Kantstrasse 12, and Hansa-Theater, Alt-Moabit 47, usually

CULTURE, ENTERTAINMENT AND NIGHTLIFE

Deutsches Theater, a national stage

have a light-hearted repertoire.

The UFA-Fabrik at Viktoriastrasse 13 is a cultural factory in Kreuzberg. Alternative Berliners swear by this venue for theatre, dance, music and film. The BELT (Berlin English Language Theatre), Stierstrasse 5, and Berlin Play Actors (also English speaking) have no fixed venue but play wherever they get a space.

East

The great Berlin theatrical tradition has always been concentrated in what became the East. The Berliner Ensemble, at Bertolt-Brecht-Platz 1, is still the official Bertolt Brecht Theatre, with a large repertoire of his work. The productions have not changed, and the theatre has been criticised for fossilisation. To newcomers it feels wonderfully atmospheric. The Volksbühne, Rosa Luxemburg-Platz, and the Deutsches Theater (where Max Reinhardt was a director), Schumannstrasse 13a–14, are other notable venues.

Film

The cinemas in the Ku'damm and around Breitscheidplatz show the latest international films. Most of them are dubbed unless they carry the letters OF (*Originalfassung* – original soundtrack) or OmU (*Originalfassung mit Untertiteln* original soundtrack with German subtitles). The best time to see international movies is during the Berlin Film Festival in February.

WEATHER & WHEN TO GO

Berlin has a continental climate, with cold, crisp winters and surprisingly hot summers. If you want to sample the *Berliner Luft* (Berlin air) in comfort, visit between April (maximum temperature in the low 70s Fahrenheit) and June (mid-80s Fahrenheit).

Weather Chart Conversion
25.4mm = 1 inch
°F = 1.8 × °C + 32

The Botanischer Garten is one of many green spaces in Berlin

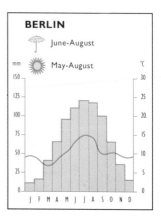

BERLIN

☂ June–August

☀ May–August

HOW TO BE A LOCAL

Berliners have a reputation for being more tolerant and relaxed than the citizens of other German cities. In the years leading up to unification, West Germans of a radical or alternative persuasion, young men wishing to avoid military service, gay people, political activists and intellectuals found a congenial home in West Berlin. The eastern sector of the city, as capital of East Germany, seemed stiff and starchy by comparison –

though it was also home to artists and intellectuals. There are many Berlin people who are by no means raving bohemians, whichever side of the one-time Wall they come from. Indeed, some may appear reserved and conservative, surrounded by a private space which seems a little greater than the usual reticence of big-city dwellers. In the months following unification, with the onset of capitalism and a release from rigid ideology, a small minority in the East began to use their new-found freedom somewhat aggressively. Racist attacks, vandalism and soccer riots all increased. If promises of economic parity fail to materialise and disappointments continue, this phenomenon will not go away. This being said, Berlin is nine times out of ten a safe and unconfrontational city, where a woman may walk unwhistled at and unmolested, free to dine alone in a restaurant without arousing comment. Mugging and personal violence is far less frequent than in London, say, or in modern Madrid. What strikes one most is how thoroughly peacable the majority appear to be – partly, perhaps, in reaction to the shocking portions of their own history, partly because they know the horrors of war as thoroughly as any group in Europe. The abhorrence of violence, both in national and personal affairs, is matched by a love of nature, a passionate attachment to green and open places. This is common to most

Germans, but it seems to be at its most intense in West Berlin in particular. People there are fiercely environmentalist, deploring not only the polluting Trabant cars which arrive from the old GDR, but also the brown coal or lignite burned in the eastern city for heating. Their passion presumably derives from the fact that for almost 50 years they were boxed inside their city, which does however have many lakes and forests within its limits.

The moment the sun shines, and even when it does not, West Berliners flock to the woods and fan out along the bicycle paths. There are any number of outings and hikes. (See the information magazines *Zitty* and *Tip* or phone the Fahrverband Wandern, the hiking association, tel: 452 4576.) The same enthusiasm for outings is shared by East Berliners, most of whom still head for the city's eastern lakes.

Though some Westerners are also beginning to head for the eastern lakes, there has so far been comparatively little crisscrossing for leisure purposes between the former East and West. This is partly because it takes time for people's habits to change. But there is the extra phenomenon of local loyalty, another matter for special fervour in Berlin. People owe allegiance to their own borough – and claim you can tell the citizens of each by their own accents – but even more so to their own tiny neighbourhood or patch of city streets, known in German as their *Kiez*.

In general, Berliners respect authority. Jaywalking is not only frowned on, it is also a fining offence. Drinking and driving is considered unacceptable. Family life is surprisingly formal. Children are not made much of, compared to those in more southerly countries. Seen and not heard appears to be the rule for public places. The time to visit family members – parents or in-laws – is for afternoon coffee on Sundays.

CHILDREN

Numerous puppet theatre groups aim their work at children, putting on shows which present no language problem for visitors. Berlin Figurentheater, Yorckstrasse 59, Fliegenotes Theater, Gneisenaustrasse 2, and the Ufa-Fabrik, Viktoriastrasse 13–18, usually have something that appeals to young people. In the East, the Puppentheater, at Greifswalder Strasse 81–4, near Ernst-Thälmann-Park, also provides shows which children who do not speak German can enjoy.

The amount of open green space in the city is a bonus for children. In the West, the Tiergarten, Grunewald woods, Teufelsberg, lakes and canals all provide some opportunity for swimming and watersports. Children's ponies can be taken out from Ponyhof Lange, Buckower Chausee 82, Marienfelde (tel: 721 6005).

Museum für Verkehr und Technik

The East is similarly blessed with green space and water. The Ernst Thälmann Pionierpark is an amusement park in the Wühlheide woods in Köpenick. From Köpenick Altstadt, there are Weisse Flotte boat trips to the Grosser Müggelsee.

In both parts of Berlin, there are plenty of swimming pools. For waterslides and wave machines, head for Blub, a waterpalace at Buschkrugallee 64 (U-Bahn Blaschko Allee)

open until midnight on weekends.

The Zoo and its aquarium are old standbys, and all the museums have something to offer children. The Museen Dahlem has a separate section which has been designed especially for children, and the Museum für Verkehr und Technik is a draw for anyone who likes computers or mechanical things.

TIGHT BUDGET

- Buy a special 24-hour Berlin ticket which gives you unlimited travel throughout the city on all buses, trams, trains and BVG ferries, but not excursion buses or private boats.
- A six-day ticket, the *Umweltkarte*, or Environment Ticket, designed to make people leave their cars at home, is obtainable from Zoo Station – even better value.
- For cheap but filling snacks, try curry sausage, bockwurst or döner kebab in the *schnell imbiss* fast food stalls.

Schnell imbiss: fast filling food

- Hostels are the cheapest places to stay (some impose a curfew, so check).
- At cheaper hotels, check whether prices include breakfast, which, if it is a sturdy one, can save the cost of a big lunch.
- For a long stay, try the Mitwohnzentrale (see **Accommodation**), which arranges apartment accommodation.

SPECIAL EVENTS

February
Berlin International Film Festival Ten days of non-stop films in venues all over the city.

April
Free Berlin Art Exhibition The city's artists display their work at the exhibition centre in the Funkturm (Kaiser-damm U-Bahn stop).

May
Berlin Drama Festival Performances throughout the city's theatres.

June
Jazz in the Garden is a four-week jazz festival, held in the gardens of the Neue Nationalgalerie. Top bands and performers.
Festival of World Cultures Held every four years (1992, 1996 etc).

July
Bach Days A musical celebration of Bach in churches and concert halls (second week of the month).
Summer Music Festival Open air jazz and modern music.

Olympic Stadium, Charlottenburg

September
Berlin Festwochen Big
jamboree of opera, music,
theatre and art throughout the
city (runs into October).

October
Jazz Festival (runs into
November).

December
The **Weinachtsmart** (Christmas
market) appears on
Breitscheidplatz and adjacent
streets, selling festive
delicacies, decorations, gifts
and the like, from 1 December
to Christmas Eve.

SPORTS

Berlin is not a particularly
athletic city although joggers
will find plenty of kindred
spirits puffing round the
Tiergarten. The Berlin
Marathon takes place on the
last Sunday in September.

West
You can roller skate at
Rollerskating-center,
Hasenheide 108, and at the ZB
Stadion Wilmersdorf, Fritz-
Wildung-Strasse. Ice skating
takes place at Eissporthalle
Berlin, Jaffestrasse (indoor
rink), and at Eisstadion Berlin-
Wilmersdorf, Fritz-Wilding-

SPORTS

Strasse 9 (outdoor). Skiing and tobogganing down the Teufelsberg are favourite activities on snowy winter weekends.

Boats can be rented on the Neuer See in Tiergarten or the Strandbad Wannsee where you can also swim in an outdoor pool. There are other swimming pools throughout the city but the largest is probably the Olympia-Schwimmstadion at Olympischer Platz. The Landesportbund, Jesse-Owens-Allee 1–2 (tel: 300 020) has full details of participator and spectator sports.

Boaters navigate the backwaters of the Tiergarten's woods

East
Volkspark Friedrichshain, Leninallee 77, has the Sport und Erholongszentrum, a leisure centre with swimming pools including one for the handicapped, saunas, solarium and bowling alley, volleyball and badminton courts, plus ice skating in the winter and roller skating in the summer. There are watersports at Langer See, near Grünau; for boating try Weisser See (Weissensee district).

Horseracing (trot races) takes place at Trabrennbahn Karlshorst, Hermann-Duncker-Strasse 129, and gallop races at Galopprennbahn Hoppegarten, Goethestrasse 1.

DIRECTORY

Contents

Arriving
Camping
Crime
Customs Regulations
Disabled Travellers
Driving
Electricity
Embassies and
 Consulates
Emergency
 Telephone
 Numbers

Entertainment
 Information
Health
Holidays
Lost Property
Media
Money Matters
Opening Times
Personal Safety
Pharmacies
Places of Worship

Police
Post Office
Public Transport
Senior Citizens
Student and
 Youth Travel
Telephones
Time
Tipping
Toilets
Tourist Offices

Arriving

By air

Flying is the quickest and most economical way to get to Berlin. The main airport for international flights is Tegel, in the West. Delta Airlines, Lufthansa, TWA and United Airlines fly direct to Tegel from New York and other North American cities. Schönefeld airport in the former East still mainly serves passengers entering from eastern European countries, the CIS and so on. A frequent bus and taxi service from Tegel takes you to the main city terminus at Bahnhof Zoologischer Garten (Zoo station) and there are coaches from Schönefeld to the west. Tegel is not in the luxury class of airports but it has all the usual facilities – exchange, duty free shops and a good phone-link hotel reservations system. There is a charge for airport security (10 DM in 1991) payable as you leave the country.

By land

Those travelling to Berlin by car have free access. If you qualify for a discount as a young person or senior citizen, travelling by train or coach may appeal; but check extra costs and journey time against air travel. Germany offers flat-rate rail tickets for unlimited travel within a specified time, and these may be available from other European countries, for all age groups.

Entry formalities

A valid passport is required by US and Canadian citizens. Nationals of other countries may need a visa.

Camping

Berlin has three camping sites for tents and campers. They are all clean, well run and cheap but not central. Contact the German National Tourist Office in your country, or get in touch with the Deutschen Camping-Clubs eV Geisbergstrasse 11, Berlin 30 (tel: 24 60 71/72).

DIRECTORY

Crime

Berlin never used to have a crime problem but easier access from the West has led to its increase – particularly muggings and car break-ins. Take the usual precautions and leave valuables and excess cash in hotel safes; do not flaunt large amounts of cash; carry money and other valuables in a secure pocket or money belt in crowded places such as markets.

Customs Regulations

Visitors from the US or Canada can take in 200 cigarettes or 25 cigars or 250 grams of tobacco, a litre of spirits and two litres of wine without paying duty. There are no currency restrictions.

Disabled Travellers

For practical help with renting wheelchairs and so on, contact Deutscher Paritätischer Wohlfahrtsverband, Brandenburgischenstrasse 80 (tel: 86 00 10).

Driving

You must have a valid driving licence. Drive on the right, pass on the left. Berliners complain about the growing density of their traffic but it is not a major problem. The speed limit on motorways is 130kmph (81mph); outside built-up areas 100kmph (62mph); and in built-up areas, 50kmph (31mph). Traffic regulations are strictly enforced, particularly in

Pleasure boats on the Wannsee

relation to speeding and use of alcohol. Fines are payable on the spot and the police may remove your car keys. At the time of German reunification the blood alcohol limit in East Germany was zero. Whatever the current situation you are advised to use public transportation rather than drinking and driving.

Car rental is *Autovermietung.* You must be over 21 and have driven for at least a year. International companies are represented at Tegel airport and major hotels.

Electricity
220 volts on a two-pin plug. Visitors from North America require a voltage transformer for appliances not fitted with dual-voltage.

Embassies and Consulates
US Clayallee 170, Berlin 33 (tel: 832 4087).
Canada Europa-Center, 1000 Berlin 30 (tel: 261 1161).
Australia Godesberger Allee 105-7, 5300 Bonn 2 (tel: (228) 81030).
United Kingdom Uhlandstrasse 7, 1000 Berlin 12 (tel: 309 5292).

Emergency Telephone Numbers
Police 110
Fire 110
Ambulance 110
Medical assistance 31 00 31

Entertainment Information
Berlin-Program is published monthly by the tourist office, listing all major events of interest to the visitor. *Tip* and *Zitty* are two listings magazines which cover absolutely

everything in all parts of the city. They come out in alternate weeks and are available at all newsstands and kiosks.

Entry Formalities
see **Arriving**

Health
No vaccinations are needed to enter Berlin. National medical insurance covers Canadian citizens while in Germany. American citizens should take out travel insurance. Berlin's health system, though somewhat bureaucratic, is quite good.

Holidays
New Year's Day: 1 January, Good Friday, Easter Monday and Ascension Day: variable dates
Labour Day: 1 May
Day of Unity: 3 October
Day of Prayer and
    Repentance: third
    Wednesday in November
Christmas: 24 December (pm), 25 and 26 December

Lost Property
The main police lost property office (Fundbüro der Polizei) is the first port of call: Platz der Luftbrücke 6 (tel: 6991). If your loss occurred on public transportation, contact the BVG at Potsdamer Strasse 184 (tel: 216 1413).
In the East, the main lost property office is on Wilhelm-Pieck-Strasse 164 (tel: 282 3472/3 or 280 6235). If you lose anything on the S-Bahn, call at the Marx-Engels-Platz S-Bahnhof (tel: 492 1671); on the U-Bahn, go to the Alexanderplatz station lost property office.

DIRECTORY

Media

Foreign newspapers and magazines are widely available in the kiosks around Zoo Station, Ku'damm and Europa-Center. Of the German press, the most substantial national dailies are *Die Welt* and *Frankfurter Allgemeine*. *Bild* is more like a tabloid. West Berlin also has two local papers – *Die Zeit* and *Tageszeitung* and six TV channels including two from the old East. Satellite services also carry television programmes produced for the Allied forces, and the visitor can pick up Allied radio programmes. The BBC World Service radio is on 90.2FM.

In the East, *Neues Deutschland* is the major national daily. Local papers are *Berliner Zeitung* and *Tageszeitung* or *TAZ*. *Junge Welt* is designed for a youthful audience. There are two East German television stations, DDR1 and 2, and five radio stations with a wideranging input from pop and serious music to drama and news.

Money Matters

There are 100 Pfennigs (Pf) in 1 Deutsche Mark (DM). Coins: 1, 2, 5, 10, 20, 50 Pf and DM 1, 2, 5. Notes: DM 10, 20, 50, 100, 500, 1000.

All banks are open Monday to Friday 9:00A.M.–1:00P.M., and most of them reopen on two weekday afternoons (usually Tuesday and Thursday), 3:30–6:00P.M., but these times vary. The Wechselstube or money exchange in Zoo Station is open Monday to Saturday 8:00A.M.–9:00P.M., and on Sundays 10:00A.M.–6:00P.M. At the Europa-Center it opens from Monday to Friday 9:00A.M.–6:00P.M., and on Saturday 9:00A.M.–4:00P.M. Exchange rates are generally more favourable at the Wechselstube.

Travelers cheques are welcomed, but credit cards are not much used except in good hotels and top restaurants. You can get a cash advance on credit cards at the money exchanges in Zoo Station and the Europa-Center.

In theory you can make the same transactions all over the city, but facilities are still limited in the East. Change money at the new 24-hour Wechselstube at Friedrichstrasse Station or use branches of the Staatsbank der DDR.

Opening Times

Shops are open from Monday to Friday 9:00A.M.–6:00P.M., and Saturday mornings 9:00A.M.–1:00P.M. Larger stores usually stay open late on one evening of the week (Thursday) and on the first Saturday of the month. Museum opening times vary although most are closed on Mondays. They remain open on all official holidays, and close the day after.

In the East museums may be shut for two days in the week, and parts may be closed off on other days for no apparent reason. Don't plan to visit museums in this part of town on a Monday. The traditional practice of cafés and bars closing down one day a week is always a surprise to visitors, but this is also changing.

Personal Safety
Berlin has always been known for the safety of its streets and public places. Things are changing in this respect with growing numbers of racist incidents (particularly in the East), but Berlin remains one of the least threatening major cities in Europe. Two areas that are best avoided late at night are Kreuzberg and the red light district around Ku'damm U-Bahn.

Pharmacies
A pharmacy is called an *Apotheke*, and keeps normal shop hours. When closed, it displays the address of the nearest open pharmacy on the door. The Europa-Apotheke, in the West, is open 9:00A.M.–9:00P.M. daily. In the East, there is a useful central pharmacy, which is situated on Alexanderplatz.

Berliner Dom's elegant cupola above the trees of Museumsinsel

Places of Worship
There are many Christian Catholic and Protestant churches as well as mosques, temples and synagogues.

Police
Berlin *Polizei* – police – wear dark green uniforms.

Post Office
Post office is *Postamt*. The Zoo Station central post office is open 24 hours a day. Branch post offices are open from Monday to Friday 8:00A.M.–6:00P.M., and Saturday mornings until noon. Mail boxes are bright yellow. In the East the main post office in the Palast der Republik at Marx-Engels-Platz opens daily from 10:00A.M. to 8:00P.M. If you are in a hurry, mail in the West.

DIRECTORY

Public Transportation

East and West have reconnected their old transportation links. A combination of buses, underground trains (U-Bahn), suburban surface trains (S-Bahn), and some ferry boats provide Berlin with an efficient public transportation system. It is administered by the Berliner

BERLIN
U-BAHN and S-BAHN

Verkehrs-Betriebe, or BVG, which has an information kiosk at Zoo Station. Services run from about 4:00 A.M. until around midnight (later on Saturday night). Night buses run a limited service. Tickets are transferable between BVG bus, train and ferry services. Single fares are expensive – it

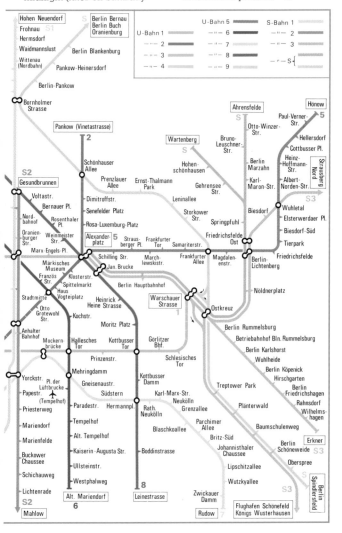

makes more sense to buy a 24-hour (or weekly) Berlin ticket, which gives unlimited travel on buses and trains. Children under six travel free; children from six to fourteen travel at reduced rates. Taxis are good value and are found at all termini and outside hotels, or can be hailed in the street. A cheap tram system operates in the East (tickets are the same as for buses). Trams have nostalgic value but are slow. There are also pleasure boat cruises on city waterways (not BVG).

Senior Citizens

Production of an identity card will secure many reductions in entrance fees, river boat tickets and the like. It is always worth asking. A rich cultural life and relatively low crime rate make this an appealing city for older travellers.

Student and Youth Travel

Two hostels are **Jugendgästehaus am Zoo**, Hardenbergerstrasse 9, and **Jugendgästehaus**, Kluckstrasse 3 (you need an International Youth Hostel Federation card for this one). You should book well ahead. Both are in the West. The Informationszentrum Hardenbergerstrasse 20, publishes a free booklet *Berlin for Junge Leute* (*Berlin for Young People*), which is useful for teenagers and upwards.

Telephones

Berlin telephone numbers have from four to eight digits, which may be grouped in various ways. International calls can be made from public telephone kiosks showing a black receiver in a green square. They take DM1, DM2 and DM5 coins. Or use the main post office at Zoo Station. Cheap rates operate during the weekend and from Monday to Friday 8:00P.M.–8:00A.M.

West

National Directory Enquiries: 1188

International Directory Enquiries: 00118

Operator: 03

International Operator: 0010

Area code for West Berlin: (0)30

To call West Berlin from the US or Canada dial 011, followed by 49 30, followed by the number. The code from West Berlin is 001 for the US and Canada.

East

Making international calls can be a lengthy process, but these facilities are being improved. Local calls pose no problems.

Operator and Directory Enquiries: 180

International Operator: 181

To call East Berlin from overseas, dial the international code above followed by 37 2, followed by the number. Consult an operator for international calls from East Berlin, and calls between East and West Berlin.

Time

Berlin is six hours ahead of US EST in winter and seven hours ahead in summer.

Tipping

A service charge – *bedienung* – is usually included in hotel and restaurant bills, but most

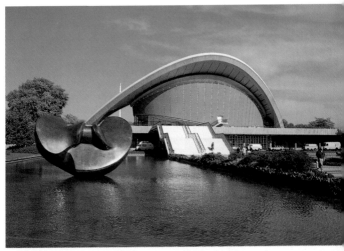

Kongresshalle, given by the US

people leave a little on top. It is usual to tip porters, maids, taxi drivers and washroom attendants.

Toilets

Public toilets usually carry the symbol of a man or woman or are labelled *Herren* (men); or *Damen* or *Frauen* (women). Most are free. Some are operated by a 10-Pf coin.

Tourist Offices

The main tourist office in former West Berlin – Verkehrsamt Berlin – is in the Europa-Center, Budapesterstrasse entrance. It is open daily 8:00A.M.–11:00P.M. (tel: 262 6031/21234). The office in Zoo Station is also open during the same hours (tel: 313 9063).

Another source of valuable information about the city, used by young people in particular, is the Informationszentrum at Hardenbergstrasse: open Monday to Friday 8:00A.M.– 7:00P.M., and Saturday 8:00A.M.–4:00P.M. It provides useful publications in English which are not available at the Verkehrsamt. In the same building, the British Centre and, next door, the Amerika Haus are both good sources of information (and solidarity, if needed) for English-speaking visitors.

In the East, the major tourist office is in the Reisebüro at Alexanderplatz 5: open: Monday to Friday 8:00A.M.– 8:00P.M., and weekends 9:00A.M.–6:00P.M. You can also change money here and reserve tickets for shows or trips. The Informationszentrum – tourist information office – beneath the Fernsehturm (TV Tower) (tel: 212 4675) will tell you what to see in the city.

Overseas

Germany has tourist offices at:
US: 747 Third Avenue, 33rd
Floor, New York, NY 10017
(tel: (212) 308 3300).
Canada: PO Box 417, 2 Fundy
Place, Bonaventure, Montreal,
Quebec H5A 1B8
(tel: (514) 878/9885).
Australia: Lufthansa House,
12th Floor, 143 Macquerie
Street, Sydney 2000
(tel: (02) 221 1008).
UK: 65 Curzon Street, London
W1Y 7PE (tel: (071) 495 3990).

Rotes Rathaus, the city hall

LANGUAGE

Many Berliners know at least a
smattering of English and many
may be fluent; but efforts to
speak German will be
appreciated. German has
some special features. The
letter ß is the same as 'ss'.
There are capital letters at the
start of all nouns; and 'the' may
be *der*, *die* or *das* depending
on whether a noun is
masculine, feminine or neuter.
If in doubt use *der*. There are
two ways to say 'you': always
use the polite 'Sie' unless told
otherwise. 'Du' is informal.

yes ja
no nein
please bitte
thanks danke
good morning/day
guten Morgen/Tag
goodbye auf wiedersehen
excuse me
entschuldigen Sie bitte
how are you?
wie geht es Ihnen?
very well, thanks; and you?
danke, gut; und Ihnen?
do you speak English?
sprechen Sie Englisch?
I don't understand
Ich verstehe nicht
My name is . . . Ich heisse . . .

Where? wo?
when? wann?
today heute
tomorrow morgen
yesterday gestern
in the morning am vormittag
in the afternoon am nachmittag
in the evening am abend

where is . . . ? wo ist . . . ?
to the left nach links
to the right nach rechts
straight ahead geradeaus

open offen
closed geschlossen
good gut
bad schlecht
big gross
small klein
expensive teuer
cheap billig
how much does it cost?
wieviel kostet es?

(the) room (das) Zimmer
(the) menu (die) Speisekarte
breakfast Frühstück
lunch Mittagessen
dinner Abendessen

**Monday, Tuesday,
Wednesday, Thursday, Friday,
Saturday, Sunday**
Montag, Dienstag, Mittwoch,
Donnerstag, Freitag,
Sonnabend, Sonntag

1 eins
2 zwei
3 drei
4 vier
5 fünf
6 sechs
7 sieben
8 acht
9 neun
10 zehn
11 elf
12 zwölf
13 dreizehn
14 vierzehn
15 fünfzehn
16 sechzehn
17 siebzehn
18 achtzehn
19 neunzehn
20 zwanzig
21 ein-und-zwanzig
30 dreissig
40 vierzig
50 fünfzig
60 sechzig
70 siebzig
80 achtzig
90 neunzig
100 hundert

INDEX

INDEX/ACKNOWLEDGEMENTS

The Automobile Association wishes to thank the following photographers and libraries for their assistance in the preparation of this book.

ADRIAN BAKER took all the photographs (© AA PHOTO LIBRARY) except:

J ALLAN CASH PHOTOLIBRARY 63 Platz der Akademie, 82/3 Schloss Sanssouci, 84 Chinese Teahouse Sanssouci.

MARY EVANS PICTURE LIBRARY 14/5 French Immigration to Berlin, 18 Cavalry attack.

NATURE PHOTOGRAPHERS LTD 88 White tailed eagle (E A Janes), 89 Common Crane (M E Gore), 90 Long-leaved sundew (P J Newman).

SPECTRUM COLOUR LIBRARY 78 Cecilienhof.

WORLD PICTURES Cover Schloss Charlottenburg.